The Perfect Ohio Lawn

Published by Cool Springs Press, a Division of Thomas Nelson, Inc., P.O. Box 141000, Nashville, Tennessee 37214.

Myers, Melinda.
    The perfect Ohio lawn : attaining and maintaining the lawn you want / Melinda Myers.
        p. cm.
    Includes bibliographical references (p.   ).
    ISBN 1-930604-34-3 (pbk. : alk. paper)
    1. Lawns—Ohio. 2. Turf management—Ohio. I. Title.
SB433.16.O3 M94 2003
635.9'647'09771—dc21

                                        2002151975

First Printing 2003
Printed in the United States of America
10 9 8 7 6 5 4 3 2 1

Managing Editor: Jenny Andrews
Horticulture Editor: Dr. Frank S. Rossi
Copyeditor: D. Michelle Adkerson
Designer: Bill Kersey
Production Artist: S.E. Anderson

Cover: top photo by Lorenzo Gunn, bottom photo by Thomas Eltzroth

Visit the Thomas Nelson website at www.ThomasNelson.com

The Perfect Ohio Lawn

Attaining and Maintaining the Lawn You Want

Melinda Myers

COOL SPRINGS PRESS

Nashville, Tennessee
A Division of Thomas Nelson, Inc.
www.ThomasNelson.com

Dedication

This book is dedicated to all the University (Cooperative) Extension specialists in Wisconsin, the Midwest, and the country who have helped me along the way. Your tireless dedication and willingness to share your knowledge and expertise do not go unnoticed.

Acknowledgments

This book, like all my others, is a compilation of my experience and education as well as the insights shared by others. It would never have been written without the support, kindness, and generosity of family, friends, and colleagues. I am always nervous to list people by name for fear of leaving someone out. I will ask your forgiveness in advance.

First, a special thanks to my daughter Nevada who shares me with gardeners, students, and all my extra projects including this book. You keep me young, grounded, laughing, and focused on what is important. To all my "adopted" children—you have expanded our family and filled our home with joy, laughter, and a little extra drama. And my husband Wes, thanks for the patience maneuvering around the piles of books, laundry, and plant samples. Our house may never be clean—but it will always be full of life.

And thanks to my parents, though miles away, your continued love and support have helped me along my journey. Thanks to my friends, near and far, who keep me moving forward and laughing when things look overwhelming. You are the best. And thanks to my sister-in-law Maryann who baled me out with last minute typing so I could meet my deadline.

Thanks to Frank Rossi, Turfgrass Professor at Cornell, and my University of Wisconsin colleagues who keep me current on turf issues and help me when I get stumped—John Stier, Chris Williamson, Phil Pellitteri, and Brian Hudelson. Thanks also to all my friends and colleagues in the horticulture profession. I am always grateful to be in a profession filled with generous people willing to share their time, talents, and expertise for the good of the cause.

And thanks to my fellow Cool Springs Press authors. Steve Dobbs of Oklahoma, thanks for the vote of confidence and for creating the framework with the Southern Lawns series so the Midwest books would go together more smoothly. Thanks to Jim Fizzell, Illinois, a long-time friend and colleague— your Illinois perspective and expertise is appreciated. And to Jo Ellen Sharp, Indiana, thanks for sharing your Indiana insight, expertise, friendship, and great ideas. And all the folks at Cool Springs Press and Thomas Nelson— thanks for the opportunity.

Contents

Foreword

Right now you may be thinking "Who is this Melinda Myers?" and "What does she know about lawns?" I always ask these questions about the author of any book I read and purchase. The answer: a horticulturist and gardener with over twenty years of experience working with grass and other landscape plants throughout Wisconsin, the Midwest, and the country.

My first lawn experience was in Ohio where I grew up. As a teenager I thought cutting the grass was a great way to get some exercise and a tan, while impressing my parents by helping around the house. I gained my professional lawn experience working with homeowners and other landscape professionals. And all the while helping home gardeners maintain the lawn of their dreams—whether it be a perfect weed-free carpet or something green to keep their feet from getting muddy when it rains.

And that is the goal of this book—helping you grow your idea of the "perfect lawn." The basics are covered in a simple, easy-to-follow manner. The detailed background information in each chapter will take the mystery out of planting and maintaining the grass, as well as managing any pest problems that develop. I find that if I understand the "why" it is much easier to do the task and do it correctly. I am hoping the same works for you. The maintenance calendar in the Introduction provides general guidelines to help you focus on the task at hand and not become overwhelmed by a season of lawn care.

Once the lawn is properly installed, we focus on—mowing, watering, and fertilizing. If done correctly, you will have minimal problems with weeds, insects, and diseases. The effort expended and resources (water and fertilizer) used will influence the quality of your lawn. Invest the maximum time and effort and you can grow a golf course quality lawn. Or invest less time and effort and have an attractive healthy lawn that complements your more informal landscape.

You will find answers and insights to commonly asked questions and challenges faced by you and other lawn gardeners throughout the Midwest. Use this book as a reference before undertaking a task, or when your lawn is in trouble and you need some advice. Either way it should help make less work of lawn care while still getting the results you want.

Have fun growing and maintaining your "Perfect Lawn."

Melinda Myers

Growing Grass in Ohio

"Variable," "unpredictable," and sometimes "extreme" describe the weather in Ohio. Some gardeners find this the exciting and challenging part of gardening. Others, frustrated by the fact that no two of the same season are exactly alike, wish for consistency and predictability. Fortunately, cool-weather grasses seem to tolerate the changeable weather better than many gardeners.

Ohio's climate is usually described as moist, temperate, and continental. But the winter and summer extremes may make you think differently. Record temperatures demonstrate this quite well. Ohio's record high was 113 degrees Fahrenheit in Gallipolis on July 21, 1934. The record low of minus 39 degrees occurred at Milligan on February 10, 1899. If you live near Lake Erie, you may sometimes feel like you live in another state. The lake keeps things a bit cooler in the summer and warmer in the winter. Then there is the lake effect snow to keep you guessing. Though extremes vary with the distance from Lake Erie and throughout the state, some general weather trends influence your lawn's health.

Springs tend to be cool and moist with fluctuating temperatures and unexpected late-spring snows. This changeable weather makes you wonder when it's safe to plant. The cool temperatures are great for the lawn, helping it green up before most plants dare to peek out of dormancy and start to grow. But lingering snow or cool, wet spring weather increases the risk of disease.

Summers are usually warm, with temperatures reaching the 80s, 90s, and even 100s. These hot spells are often interrupted by weather fronts that bring summer showers or thunderstorms and cooler temperatures. Extreme heat and drought can be tough on you and your lawn. Cool-season grasses go dormant and may turn brown during these extremes. Unfortunately, most weeds and insects don't. Keeping the grass tall and healthy helps it ward off pests and survive these difficult times.

Fall really has the best weather for lawn grasses. The cool air temperatures help your lawn recover from the heat and drought of summer. This, combined with shorter days, means the grass plants focus on root and shoot development instead of just growing tall. This helps the lawn prepare for winter and means a bit less mowing for you.

Winter brings cold temperatures and snow. Lawns naturally cease growing during cold weather and may turn brown. Snowfall can vary from a light dusting to several feet. It may last for weeks or even months or disappear as quickly as it arrived. And we all know about the unexpected fall or spring snows that remind us that nature is truly in control.

Soils

Good soil is the foundation for a beautiful healthy lawn. Some gardeners are lucky enough to start with well-drained soils made of a good mixture of organic matter, sand, silt, and clay. But most of us are stuck with poorly drained soils loaded with clay or with sandy soils that dry out too quickly.

Ohio's climate and geography have influenced the development of our soils and what ended up in your garden. The more recent history of building and construction has added its mark and greatly changed our native soil. In fact, many horticulturists don't call it "soil"—and they refer to planting areas as "disturbed sites." This means you have a lot of work to do.

Let's start with a look at history. Much of Ohio was covered with glaciers at one time. As the glaciers receded, they left behind a mix of rock, sand, silt, and clay particles. Northeastern Ohio and areas along Lake Erie tend to be fertile. The western part of the state is the most fertile farmland and marks the beginning of the corn belt. The eastern part of the state starts with rolling hills in the north and changes to rugged hills and valleys in the south. Soil pH varies from 2.0 in strip mine areas of the southeast, 5.0 in eastern and southeastern regions, and a high pH, up to 8.0, in central, western, and north-western Ohio.

The climate and geology created some good growing soils—that is, until we started building houses, roads, and parking lots. All the construction moved and transformed much of our soil. As a result, you find great variability even in your own yard.

The best way to identify your soil type and develop a management plan is with a soil test. See Chapter One for tips on taking a soil test and using its results. Contact your local University Extension Service for information on where to send the sample for analysis. Creating a maintenance plan based on your unique soil is the best way to grow a healthy and attractive lawn with the least amount of effort.

Hardiness

This word is often associated with the people, as well as the plants, of the Midwest. Hardiness zones reflect the average minimum winter temperature for that area. A plant's hardiness is the coldest area in which the plant can survive. Ohio contains mostly Zones 6a through 5a, with small sections of 6b on the borders of Ohio and West Virginia and Kentucky.

Most of the southern region of the state (Zone 6a) has milder winters, with average minimum winter temperatures of minus 5 to minus 10 degrees Fahrenheit. The northern part of the state is Zone 5b, with fingers of this colder zone reaching into the south. Average minimum winter temperatures are minus 15 to minus 10 degrees. A few islands of Zone 5a are scattered throughout the northern half of the state. There, the minimum winter temperatures are minus 20 to minus 15 degrees. Lake Erie affects temperatures, with a warmer area (Zone 6a) along its shoreline.

Fortunately, all the cool-season grasses survive and thrive throughout the state. The lawn goes dormant and may turn brown during cold winter weather but recovers as warmer temperatures return.

Heat hardiness is a relatively new rating for the country and our plants. This hardiness rating is based on maximum summer temperatures. The country was divided into regions based on the number of days that temperatures reach at least 86 degrees Fahrenheit during the growing season—the temperature at which plants can suffer injury. Plant damage due to heat stress can be more subtle than cold. Different parts of the plants may be affected at different times and in different ways. The overall plant may be stunted or withered.

The United States' twelve heat zones range from Zone 1, which averages less than one heat day (temperatures of at least 86 degrees Fahrenheit) to Zone 12, which has more than 210 heat days. See the American Horticulture Society's website (http://www.ahs.org/publications/heat_zone_map.htm) for more information on heat hardiness and a look at the heat hardiness map for the U.S.

Ohio contains Heat Zones 6 through 4. The southern one-fourth of the state (Zone 6) typically experiences forty-five to sixty days of at least 86 degrees. The central and northwestern regions are rated Zone 5, with thirty to forty-five days of at least 86 degrees. The northeast is the coolest region, Zone 4, with fourteen to thirty heat days. Islands of cooler and warmer zones are scattered throughout the larger heat zones.

Most cool-weather grasses survive Ohio's summers by going dormant and sometimes turning brown during hot dry weather. This is the plant's natural defense mechanism. Watering the lawn will delay dormancy, but in extreme heat, even watered lawns may go dormant. Keep the grass tall, and don't fertilize or apply weed killers during the hot dry summer weather.

Precipitation

Water is one of the key factors in growing a healthy and attractive lawn, and nature provides most of the water your lawn needs. As you can see on the precipitation map at the end of this introduction, northern Ohio receives about 30 inches and southern Ohio receives about 40 inches of rain each year, while the central part receives 35 to 40 inches annually. But the total amount of precipitation tells only part of the story.

What really determine the health and appearance of your lawn are the amount and frequency of rainfall. Most Ohio lawns receive 3 inches of rain each month. Mid- to late summer often brings hot dry spells that can last for several weeks. The grass goes dormant to survive the drought. Supplemental water is needed to keep it green during drought. Your desire and ability to water influence the look of your lawn throughout the summer. Fortunately, properly maintained lawns can survive most Ohio droughts.

Find out how your backyard compares to the rest of the state. Invest in a rain gauge or make your own from a straight-sided can. Check weekly rainfall, and adjust your watering and management practices to fit the weather. See Chapter Two for more information about watering your lawn.

Maintenance

Keep your grass healthy with proper mowing, watering, and fertilization. The quality of grass desired and the amount of use it receives influence the amount of work and resources you need to invest. A golf-course quality lawn requires more frequent mowing, fertilization, watering, and aeration. Play areas may need overseeding, aeration, and a little more fertilizer to keep them looking good despite the constant wear. But a lawn that is viewed, not used, or seen as a ground cover to complement other plantings may require minimal care.

Use the Ohio Turf Maintenance at a Glance chart at the end of this introduction to see what lawn-care tasks need to be done and when. Use this as a starting point to develop your own management plan, one that allows you to grow the lawn you desire. Consult the fertilization chart at the end of this introduction, and select the schedule that best fits your maintenance goals. Keep monitoring your lawn's health and vigor, and make needed adjustments throughout the season and over time.

A bit of well-directed effort can give you the results you want. Coming chapters detail such issues as watering, mowing, fertilizing, and managing pests in your Ohio lawn.

For More Information

This book provides the basics you need to get your lawn started and growing, and to keep it healthy. But all gardeners know that surprises occur. Contact your local University Extension Service if you need additional information. They have excellent publications, staff, and master gardeners to help you with your lawn questions. Some services are free, while others, such as publications, may have a minimal fee.

Check the government section of your phone book for the phone number and address of your local Extension Office. It is often listed as "Extension," "Cooperative Extension," or "University Extension" under your local County Government or land grant university. Or visit the U.S. Department of Agriculture website (www.reeusda.gov), which provides links to every state and county office and can guide you to the extension resources in your region.

Many extension services provide their information on-line. Other Midwest extension services may have additional information that can help you grow your lawn and landscape. Look for sites that end in "edu." This indicates that the information is provided by a university or other educational resource. Also look for information from professional organizations or research facilities that deal with lawns. Visit www.paturf.org/links.htm for links to these and other turfgrass-related sites.

USDA Cold Hardiness Zones

ZONE	Avg. Min. Temp. Degrees Fahrenheit
5a	-15 to -20
5b	-10 to -15
6a	-5 to -10
6b	0 to -5

Total Annual Precipitation

Inches

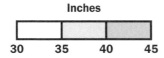

30   35   40   45

Data from the "Midwestern Regional Climate Center, Champaign, Illinois"

Turf Maintenance at a Glance

Establishment—

Seeding and Renovation—Fall (best time) August 15 to September 15 or in spring before soil temperatures reach 50 degrees

Sodding—When sod is available and the ground isn't frozen

Fertilization—See Fertilization Programs on page 15

Watering—All season, only as needed*

Aeration—September or October is best or spring (done only if needed)

Soil Test—Anytime ground isn't frozen and the lawn has not been recently fertilized

Insect and Disease Management—

Scouting—March through November (watch for subtle changes)

Watch for Snowmold—February/March/April (as snow recedes)

Watch for Fungal Diseases—April through November

Watch for Insects—May through October

Pre-emergent Herbicide for crabgrass and other weeds—April when soil temperatures reach 50 degrees (done only if needed)

Post-emergent Herbicide for broadleaf weeds—September (best time) or May (done only if needed)

Post-emergent for difficult weeds such as violets and ground ivy—Late October/November

*Supplement rainfall as needed. Water thoroughly when the grass wilts and footprints remain. This is about 1 inch of water per week. You may need more in the heat of summer and less in cooler temperatures of spring and fall.

Maintain a healthy turf and you can reduce the time, energy, and chemicals needed to control weeds, insects, and diseases. If a pesticide is used, be sure to read and follow all label directions carefully.

Fertilization Programs

Maintenance Level	Timing	lbs./1000sq. ft. (sun)	lbs/1000 sq. ft. (shade)
Low	Halloween	1	$^1/_2$
Medium	Mother's Day	$^1/_2$	$^1/_2$
	Labor Day	1	$^1/_2$
	Halloween	1	
High	Mother's Day	1	$^1/_2$
	4th of July*	1	$^1/_2$
	Labor Day	1	$^1/_2$
	Halloween	1	$^1/_2$

*Apply only if lawn is actively growing and watered during hot summer months; use fertilizers composed mostly of slow-release nitrogen.

Planning and Starting a New Lawn

Chapter One

Survey the Site

Test the Soil

Observe Shading Patterns

Prepare the Site

Planting Seed or Sod

Post-Planting Care

Renovating Existing Lawns

Site Survey

Some people view lawns as the canvas on which to create their colorful landscape of trees, shrubs, and flowers. The large expanses or curving ribbons of green grass provide unity in the landscape. Others view lawns more as a functional part of the landscape. Grass makes a good surface for play areas and keeps their feet from getting muddy when it rains. No matter what your focus, a healthy lawn is the best way to achieve your goal.

Unfortunately, we don't always start out with a healthy lawn, or good growing conditions to build a new one. Lawns and landscapes are often an afterthought for many builders, contractors, and even homeowners. The topsoil is scraped off the site and sold, the basement is dug, and the subsoil is spread over the property. Heavy clay and other aggregate materials are often hauled in and packed down to prepare the home's foundation. Leftover piles of sand, roofing materials, lumber, limestone, concrete, wire, nails, and even a few sack lunches may be buried just below the soil surface. At best, a couple of inches of topsoil are used to cover this mess and start a lawn. Grass is tough, but you are still asking a lot of any plant to grow and thrive in such conditions.

Dig a few holes in the area you want to plant, and see what you find. If the soil is full of debris or so compacted it is difficult to penetrate, you have a few problems to correct. The best approach, though usually not practical or possible, is to remove compacted fill and debris from the lawn and landscape areas, then bring in good topsoil. Use a loam soil or a blended mix that contains minerals and organic matter to create the new planting surface. Or apply a 2- to 3-inch layer of topsoil and mix into the existing soil. Then spread an additional 2 to 3 inches of soil over the area to be seeded or sodded. Be careful not to bury tree roots and trunks. Adding as little as an inch of soil can weaken and even kill some trees. Gently grade the soil away from your home's foundation. This will help keep water out of the basement and prevent future drainage problems. Make the final grade 1 inch below the sidewalk and driveway.

If bringing in good topsoil is not an option, incorporate as much organic matter as possible into your existing soil. Organic matter includes decaying plant materials or composted manures that enrich and loosen soil, improve the drainage of clay soils, hold water and nutrients in sandy soils, slow down erosion, and provide a favorable environment for earthworms and beneficial microorganisms. As it decays, organic matter releases small amounts of nutrients back into the soil for plants to use. Peat moss, composted manure, and compost are some of the most common forms of organic material. Using a tiller to add 2 to 4 inches of organic matter to the top 6 to 8 inches of soil can greatly improve any poor, nutrient-deficient soil.

Soil Testing

Soil is the foundation of a healthy lawn and landscape. Poor infertile soil means poor non-productive plants. Get your lawn off to a healthy start by improving your soil's fertility and drainage. Since turfgrass receives its primary nutrition from the soil, having your soil tested is a must. Otherwise you are "growing by guessing," and that can be costly—financially, nutritionally, and environmentally. A soil test measures the fertility of your soil and tells you what needs to be added.

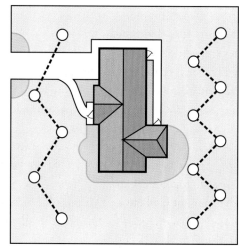

Collect separate samples from front and back lawn areas.

Take soil sample 4 to 6 inches deep.

But your soil test report is only as good as the sample you take. For best results, collect separate samples from the front and backyards. Or at least take separate samples from any problem areas. Collect at least four to six plugs of soil, 4 to 6 inches deep, from each area to be tested. Mix all the plugs from one area together, and place one to two cups in a plastic bag. Call your local Cooperative Extension Office for details on how to submit a soil sample for testing. Some county offices prefer you bring the sample into their office while others provide a mailer for sending the sample directly to the State Soils Lab. There is usually a small fee for this service, but the money spent for soil testing will be returned several times over because of the time and money you will save on fertilizer, maintenance, and pest management. Soil test results will be mailed to you in several weeks. The results will tell you about the nutrient level, organic matter, and pH of your soil and suggest what you need to add to encourage healthy plant growth.

Add the recommended phosphorous, lime, sulfur, and potassium to the soil. Spread it over the soil surface, along with the organic matter, and till it into the top 6 to 8 inches of soil. This places these slow-moving materials at the root zone where they are needed. Organic and slow-release nitrogen can be added at the same time. Wait until just before seeding to add any fast-release forms of nitrogen.

Shade or Not

Matching your grass selection to your growing conditions is a key factor in developing a good lawn. Kentucky bluegrass, fine fescues, and turf-type perennial ryegrass are the major lawn grasses for the Midwest. These hardy, cool-weather grasses stay green the majority of the year. They may brown during the extreme cold of winter and heat of summer but put on a good show the rest of the year.

Bluegrass has a fine texture and good green color. It is best suited for sunny locations. Fescues look similar but are more tolerant of shade and drought than bluegrass. Use a mixture of these two grasses for lawns with a variety of sun and shade conditions. A sunny grass seed mix contains a higher percentage of bluegrass while a shade mix contains more fescue. Both types of mix include ryegrass for quick cover and establishment.

Evaluate the sun and shade conditions in your yard. Check the yard several times a day and throughout the growing season. Keep in mind that buildings, trees, shrubs, and other structures can create shade. Use a shade mixture in areas receiving four to six hours daily of dappled or light shade. Consider using a shade-tolerant ground cover or decorative mulch in heavily shaded areas. Pave or mulch heavily used pathways.

Preparing the Planting Site

Proper soil preparation is important whether you seed or sod your lawn. Only work the soil when it is moist, not wet. Take a handful of soil and gently squeeze it, then tamp with your finger. If it stays in a mud ball, it is too wet to work. Wait a few days for the soil to dry before tilling. Tilling wet soil ruins its structure and drainage. If the soil is like dust, it is too dry to work. Tilling dry soil pulverizes it and ruins its structure. Either water the soil, or wait for a rain and repeat the test.

Using chemical or mechanical means, eliminate all weeds or grasses. Each method has benefits and drawbacks, so select the one that best fits your gardening philosophy, timeframe, and growing conditions.

Mechanical: If you have time and prefer not to use chemicals, you can mechanically remove weeds by digging, hoeing, or smothering them. Many organic gardeners have found that the black plastic method works well. That is, after organic matter is added and the rough grading is completed, cover the area with black plastic. Leave it covered for at least three months (preferably

Be aware of sunlight patterns in your yard. An area with dappled shade will limit the type of lawn you can grow there. Fescues are shade tolerant, while Kentucky bluegrass is a better grass for sunny areas.

longer) before planting. The black plastic prevents the sunlight from reaching the existing grass and weeds, so the plants eventually die. Remember the yellow grass under the kids' pool last summer? This is the same idea used over a longer period so the plants won't recover. The build-up of heat under the plastic also helps kill weed seeds near the soil surface.

Tilling to remove existing vegetation has limited success with plants like quack grass that form rhizomes (underground stems). Tilling cuts the rhizomes into small pieces and scatters them throughout the area; later, they will root and grow. So tilling actually propagates, rather than destroys, these types of plants. Tilling also brings more weed seeds to the surface. Some gardeners and landscapers have had success with continual cultivation over one or two seasons. They till the soil once a month for the first season. Often they plant a green manure crop such as winter rye to prevent erosion over winter, and then repeat the process the following summer until the lawn is seeded in the fall. They add needed organic matter to the soil in one of the final tillings. The continual cultivation keeps uprooting the unwanted plants so they eventually run out of stored energy and die. But two seasons is a long time to go without a lawn. Plus the risk of erosion, potential damage to soil structure, and loss of organic matter due to constant tilling are big disadvantages to this technique.

Chemical: Do not use pre-emergent herbicides before reseeding your lawn. These products are designed to prevent seed germination, and they will prevent your newly planted grass seed from germinating. Check the label for waiting times from application to seeding. Tupersan (siduron) has the shortest waiting period.

Chemical approaches using very specific herbicides are often the most complete eradication methods. To kill all existing vegetation, use a nonselective herbicide like glyphosate (the active ingredient in herbicides such as Roundup®) or glufosinate-ammonium (the active ingredient in the herbicide Finale®) according to label directions. "Nonselective" means the herbicide can kill anything green that the spray reaches. Since nonselective herbicides break down quickly in the soil, you can replant once the vegetation is completely dead. Check the label for the exact waiting time between application and planting. Spray herbicides far enough in advance of planting to allow the chemicals time to kill the entire plant, roots and all.

Persistent weeds or grasses such as quack grass may require several applications. Treat the area, and wait for persistent weeds to resprout and new seeds to germinate and grow. Treat the area again once the weeds are up and actively growing. You may want to treat the area then add the needed organic matter as you do the final grading. Allow the soil to settle, and wait for any persistent weeds or seeds to sprout before the final application of herbicide.

Remove large rocks, pebbles, or soil clods that may interfere with seed establishment. Large pieces of wood, tree branches, and bark should also be removed since they can contribute to a perplexing problem in lawns called "fairy ring and mushrooms," discussed in detail in Chapter Seven. Once all vegetation is killed or removed, lightly work the top inch or so of soil just before planting by tilling very shallowly or raking by hand. Working the soil too deeply will stir up more weed seeds.

Other Considerations

Irrigation systems are gaining popularity throughout the country, even in the Midwest where water is usually plentiful. The problem is that water is often not available at the time or in the amount needed by our lawns. We will talk about minimizing water use in the next chapter. Consider adding an irrigation system if you plan on watering your lawn to keep it green all season long. Installing an irrigation system can ensure that your lawn receives the right amount of water at the right time—even when you are busy or away from the garden. It can also help conserve water by allowing you to water at the most efficient time and by regulating the amount you apply based on plant needs and the weather.

Design is probably the most important step in the process. A well-designed irrigation system will meet your needs and those of your lawn. Talk with your irrigation professional to discuss your gardening style, budget, various types of plants in your landscape, and the different areas—lawn and planting beds—you plan to irrigate. This allows the irrigation professional to design a system that provides the proper amount of water to the various types of plants, not just your grass, in a timely fashion that fits the soil and weather in your area. Finding a professional to do any job can be overwhelming. Check the yellow pages for companies that can design and install irrigation systems. Ask about their training, professional affiliations, and references from past customers. Shop around to get the best quality job for a reasonable price. After all, you want this investment to last the life of your lawn.

Seed or Sod

Start your new lawn from seed or sod. Seed mixes give you a wider variety of grasses and cultivars to choose from. Seeding is cheaper than laying sod but requires a bit more time to get the lawn established. I find seeded lawns have fewer pest problems since the wide variety of seed mixes allows you to better match the grass to the growing conditions. Plus the top and bottom of the plant develop together, creating more balanced growth.

Sod allows you to have an instant lawn. Growers usually select the best varieties and some even have shade mixes. It is more expensive but takes less time to get an established lawn. Some gardeners sod the front and seed the back to save money while getting faster curb appeal. No matter which method you choose, proper soil preparation and post-planting care are critical to success.

Grass	Minimum Seed Germination	Minimum Purity
Kentucky Bluegrass	75–80%	90–95%
Fine Fescue	80–85%	95–97%
Perennial Ryegrass	90–95%	95–98%
Tall Fescue	85–90%	95–98%

For seeding, read the label carefully when selecting your grass seed. Spending a few extra dollars now can save you lots of frustration and time spent filling in bare spots, treating diseases, and managing other problems that could have been avoided. Purchase seeds with a high rate of germination. The higher the percentage, the more viable (living) seeds are in the mix. The purity rate tells you what percentage of the mix is grass seed. The remainder includes seeds from other grasses, weeds, dirt, and chaff. A high percent of purity means you are getting more grass seeds and fewer unwanted ingredients for your money.

Select a mix with several quality cultivars of each type of grass seed. This increases disease resistance and reduces the risk of losing your whole lawn to a pest infestation. Use a straight bluegrass mix for new lawns with no trees or shade-producing structures. A sunny mix, 60 percent bluegrass, 30 percent fine fescue, and 10 percent turf-type perennial ryegrass, is your best choice for lawns with minimal shade. Try shade mixes with a greater percentage of shade-tolerant fine fescue (60 percent) and less of the sun-loving bluegrass (30 percent) for partially shaded lawns.

Spread the seed with a rotary or drop-type spreader used for fertilizing the lawn. Seed sunny grass seed mixes at a rate of 3 to 4 pounds per 1,000 square feet and shady mixes at a rate of 4 to 5 pounds per 1,000 square feet. Sow half the seed in one direction and the other half at a right angle to the first. This will provide uniform coverage and avoid bare spots. Lightly rake so the seed is barely covered with soil. It needs some light to germinate. Use an empty roller to firm the soil, tamp the seed in place, and provide even more seed-to-soil contact. Never work wet or waterlogged soils; doing so increases compaction and interferes with seed germination. Use the soil moisture test, described earlier in this chapter, before working the soil.

Seed Application Pattern

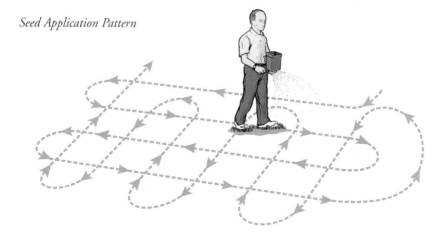

Mulch your newly seeded lawn with weed-free straw or marsh hay, one of the new cellulose-type products, or floating row covers. This helps conserve moisture and minimize erosion. A bale of straw or marsh hay, weighing between 60 and 80 pounds, will cover 1,000 square feet at a 1- to $1^1/_2$-inch thickness. Most of this will break down and can be left in place after the lawn fills in.

Check the label of other mulch products for their coverage area. The cellulose pellets are spread over the surface and watered in place to create a mulch layer. The season-extending fabrics sold as GrassFast® or Remay are spread over the newly seeded area and anchored with stones, boards, or wire pins. These fabrics let air, light, and water through while keeping the seedbed warm and safe from seed-eating birds.

Hydro-seeding is another option. You may have seen this operation used on hillsides along the freeway or other rights-of-way. Landscape professionals use a machine to apply a mixture of seed, water, and mulch to the prepared soil. This mix can be applied quickly with very good results. It is especially useful on steeply sloped areas that are more subject to erosion and wash-out during heavy rains.

Water newly seeded lawns. Moisten the soil surface and repeat often enough to keep it moist but not soggy.

Sod is just a collection of grass plants. The farmer gets the grass growing, then harvests the turf, roots and all, cuts it into manageable sizes, then rolls, stacks, and delivers it on pallets to you or your local garden center. Sod gives you an instant lawn at a cost—but it is fifteen times more effective than a seeded lawn at controlling runoff.

Select high-quality sod that is deep green and has $^1/_2$- to $^3/_4$-inch uniformly thick roots growing in moist soil. Avoid sod rolls that show signs of insects, disease, weeds, or moisture stress. Most sod is grown in full sun on highly organic soils. It contains all or mostly bluegrass plants and is best suited for sunny areas. Try to purchase sod grown on soils more like those in your yard to speed establishment and minimize transplant stress.

The traditional sod rolls are $1^1/_2$ feet wide by 6 feet long and will cover 9 square feet of soil. Divide the square footage of your lawn by nine to calculate the number of sod rolls you need to buy. For example, if you have 3,500 square feet of lawn to cover, you need 388 (3,500 divided by 9) rolls of sod. A big sod roll measures 30 inches wide by 90 feet long and covers 25 square yards. These large rolls are used for athletic fields and large commercial and residential lawns. The size and weight of this sod requires a professional and special equipment to install.

Order the sod to be delivered or pick it up just before installation. Store it in a cool shady location to prevent overheating and drying of the roots. For best results, install it as soon as possible on properly prepared soil. Give the sod special care if it must be stored for longer periods. Unroll the sod, spread it out in a shady area, and water often enough to keep the roots moist.

Start laying sod parallel to the driveway, walkway, curb, or other straight edge. Lay the first row of sod next to the longest of these straight edges. Do not pull or stretch the sod, since it has a tendency to shrink as it dries. Butt the sod ends and edges together to avoid bare areas between rolls. Stagger the seams as if you were laying bricks. Place sod perpendicular to the slope on steep hills. Use short wooden stakes or sod pins to hold this sod in place.

Sod Placement

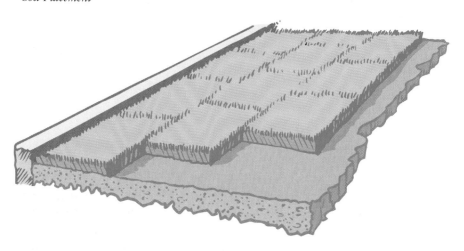

Run an empty lawn roller over the sod to eliminate air pockets and ensure good root-to-soil contact. Push the roller perpendicular to the direction the sod was laid. Water the sod immediately and thoroughly enough to moisten the top 3 to 4 inches of soil.

When to Plant Your Lawn

Late summer through early fall is the best time to seed lawns in the Midwest. The soil is warm, so the seeds sprout quickly. The air temperatures are cooler and more favorable for grass growth and establishment. Cooler temperatures mean the soil stays moist longer, making your job a bit easier. Mid- to late spring after the soil has begun to warm is the next best time to seed. The still-cool temperatures mean it will take a bit longer for the seeds to germinate, and variable spring temperatures, heavy spring rains, and the upcoming hot summer weather make it more challenging to establish a spring-planted lawn.

Avoid seeding lawns during the hot days of summer. You will waste a lot of time and water trying to grow and establish a cool-weather grass during hot weather. Many gardeners try dormant seeding in late fall. They prepare the soil and sow the seed in early winter when soil temperatures drop below 45 degrees Fahrenheit. The goal is to get the seed in place and hold it in a dormant state until the following spring. It usually doesn't work that way. Unexpected warm spells raise soil temperatures enough for the seeds to sprout, then the next cold snap kills the seedlings just as they start growing. If you feel lucky or like a challenge, you can give this a try. Don't worry about the snow; it makes the perfect winter mulch.

Sod can be laid anytime the ground isn't frozen and sod is available for sale. For best results, lay sod in spring or fall. The cool weather and warmer soils result in faster rooting and less work (watering) for you.

Post-Establishment Care

Continue to water sodded lawns often enough to keep the sod roots and soil surface moist. Reduce water frequency once the sod starts to root into the soil below. Moisten the top 3 to 4 inches of soil to encourage deep rooting. Aerate well-rooted sod to prevent future problems. If you prepared your soil properly, you incorporated the needed nutrients before planting. If not, wait until the next recommended fertilization application date to apply the needed nutrients.

Begin cutting the grass as soon as it reaches the normal mowing height—one-third taller than the normal height for your lawn. So if you keep your grass 3 inches tall, cut it when it is 4 inches tall. See Chapter Four for more on mowing and Chapter Six for guidelines on specific grasses. Removing smaller portions of the grass leaves is less stressful on the lawn and encourages more vigorous growth and deeper roots. Use a sharp blade, and do not cut the grass when it is wet. Wet leaf blades are more likely to mat together or tear and pull the plants, roots and all, right out of the ground.

Pull or dig weeds as soon as they appear. Proper watering and mowing will help your lawn to establish quickly and out-compete the weeds. Avoid general applications of herbicides (weed-killers) for at least one year after seeding. These products can weaken, damage, and even kill tender seedlings. If you use a chemical, be sure to read and follow all label directions carefully.

Renovating a Lawn

"Renovation" is used to get poorly performing lawns reestablished and back into shape. There are different levels of renovation. Partial renovation may be a simple process of seeding over thinning grass. Complete renovation is the most extreme form—it basically means starting over from scratch. Some form of renovation is usually required when a lawn becomes thin and spotty or overgrown with 50 percent or more of undesirable weeds and grasses or 5 to 10 percent quack grass.

First, find the cause of your lawn's problem. If the issue is pests, then properly identify them and treat the lawn accordingly. Pests are covered extensively in Chapter Seven. Many thinning, weed-infested lawns are the result of improper management or cultural practices. Take a soil test to determine if the problem is poor soil nutrition or improper pH. If the soil is compacted from heavy foot traffic or repetitious mowing patterns, then it may be necessary to aerate or amend the soil. This is covered in Chapter Four.

If correcting these problems does not help reestablish your existing grass, then overseeding or replanting may be required. Choose the appropriate grass types and cultivars for your site and growing conditions. Over-seed thin lawns to fill in bare spots, increase grass density, and crowd out weeds. Cut the grass as short as possible for over-seeding. It will act as living mulch for the grass seed. Remove thatch (see Chapter Four) to improve the growing conditions and ensure good seed-to-soil contact using a vertical mower (de-thatching machine) or core aerator. Rake, remove, and compost any thatch, and break up the soil cores and leave them on

Lawns not only provide recreational space and accent landscape beds, they also control erosion, reduce glare and noise, absorb air pollution, and trap dust particles.

the soil surface. Or rent a slit seeder, or hire a professional to do the job for you. Slit seeders slice a slit in the soil and drop the seed in place. This ensures good seed-to-soil contact and increases germination rates.

Spread the seed over the de-thatched or aerated lawn using a drop or rotary spreader. Apply half the recommended rate in one direction and the other half at right angles to the first. Rake to ensure the seed makes good contact with the soil surface. As the seedlings grow, raise the mowing height back to the normal 3 to $3^{1}/_{2}$ inches. Cut the grass when it reaches 4 inches tall.

Total replacement can be done in small areas or across the entire lawn depending on the extent of the problem. In either case, use the same procedures described earlier in the chapter. Kill all the existing vegetation before replanting, especially if another invasive lawn species has encroached into the preferred lawn grass. Test and prepare the soil, adding needed organic matter and fertilizers. Seed or sod, and provide the proper care to get your renovated lawn off to a good start.

Watering

Chapter Two

> **Know Your Soil Type**
>
> **Let Your Grass Tell You When to Water**
>
> **Water Deeply and Less Often**
>
> **Water Early**
>
> **Water Efficiently**
>
> **Condition Your Lawn for Drought**

Water-Holding Capacity of Soils

Weather, soil, and the type of grass you grow influence the amount and frequency of watering required. Obviously, the hotter the weather, the more frequently you need to water. Heavier soils with more organic matter require watering less often. A closer look at soil will help you do a better job of watering your lawn.

Soil is composed of mineral particles of various shapes and sizes, with water and air spaces in between. The largest and heaviest particles are sand, which holds neither nutrients nor water. Silt particles are smaller and more angular, while clay particles are mostly flat and charged, allowing them to hold onto nutrients.

Your soil's texture (its proportions of sand, silt, and clay) and its proportion of organic matter influence its ability to hold water. Sandy soils drain quickly. Try pouring a glass of water through a pile of sand—the liquid quickly disappears. Now pour water into a hole dug in clay soil. It drains much more slowly.

A soil test can tell you the texture of your soil. If you didn't do a soil test before the lawn was installed, it's not too late. Take a trowel and collect soil samples from throughout the lawn. Send the combined samples to the state's soil-testing lab for analysis. The results will tell you what type of soil you have, as well as your soil's fertilizer needs.

You can also determine your soil's texture by touch and feel. Squeeze a handful of moist soil through your index finger and thumb. Coarse soils with a high proportion of sand particles feel rough and gritty and barely hold together. Loam soils (a mix of sand, silt, and clay) are less gritty and hold together when wet. Heavy soils with a high proportion of clay are smooth and sticky and can be molded when wet.

Further evaluate your soil's drainage. Remove both ends from a large coffee can and pound it into the ground. Fill it with water. Measure the depth of the water and record the time. Measure and record the depth of the water every hour. Well-drained soils lose about an inch of water an hour. Those draining more slowly need some work.

Simple Home Test to Determine Soil Makeup

Check your soil's texture to give you a better idea of the frequency and amount of water needed to maintain your lawn. Estimate the percentages of the three main mineral components—sand, silt, and clay. A balance of the three create loamy soils, which are ideal for most plants, including turf. A simple test to determine your soil texture is based on the weight of these mineral particles when settled out of a water suspension. Sand is larger and heavier than silt, and silt is heavier than clay. The particles of each settle at various levels and times because of their different weights. This enables you to gauge the percentages of each in a soil sample.

Try this simple test—and be sure to include the whole family. I find kids have a good time "testing their soil." This may be just the trick to get them involved with lawn care. Collect several cups of soil from throughout the yard. Remove any rocks, roots, or sticks. Break up any clods to speed up the process. Now fill a quart jar two-thirds full of water and add one teaspoon of a non-foaming detergent. This will act as a wetting agent (also available in some garden centers) to separate the various soil particles.

Home test to determine soil texture.

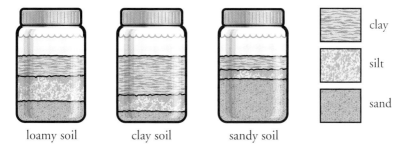

loamy soil   clay soil   sandy soil

Cover the jar and shake vigorously for several minutes until the soil particles are completely mixed with the water. Set the jar on a level surface. The largest and heaviest sand particles will settle at the bottom of the jar in about forty seconds. With a permanent marker, mark this level on the outside of the jar. The water will still be cloudy since the silt and clay particles remain suspended.

Leave the jar undisturbed for four hours. By then most of the lighter and smaller silt particles will have settled. Mark the silt layer. After twenty-four hours, the water should be clear, and the smallest and lightest particles will have settled. Mark your clay level.

Compare thicknesses of each layer. If they are about equal, you have a loamy soil. If the thicknesses differ, estimate the percentage of total space occupied by each layer (the total should equal one hundred). Now match the percentages of sand, silt, and clay to the numbers on the sides of the Soil Texture Triangle shown. Follow the directional lines into the triangle. The points of intersection show your soil texture category.

Soil Texture Triangle

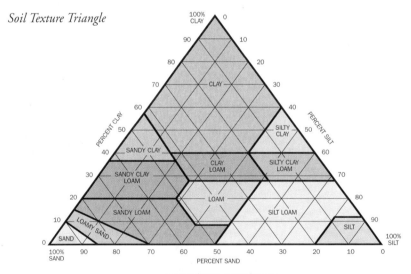

Source: Soil Science Society of America

For example, suppose your jar of soil came to 20 percent sand, 70 percent silt, and 10 percent clay. At the bottom of the diagram, which is sand, you would follow the line for 20 up and to the left. On the right, or silt, side, mark 70 and follow the line down. The remaining 10 would be located on the left, or clay side, so follow the line straight across to the right. In this example the three lines come together under "silt loam." So the soil make-up is primarily silt loam, which has fairly good water-holding capacity but is prone to compaction.

Now that you know your soil texture, you have a better idea of how often you need to water. Soils with a high percentage of sand tend to dry out quickly, while those with more clay tend to drain poorly and stay wet longer. Increasing the organic matter in the soil improves drainage in heavy clay soils and increases the water-holding capacity of sandy soils.

It's Time to Water

Let your lawn tell you when to water. No, it won't say "water me" (although that would be nice), but you can gauge your lawn's need for water by sight. Grass is 75 to 80 percent water (grass clippings are almost 90 percent water by weight). As a result, the plants show obvious signs of drought stress that help you determine when it's time to water.

The grass foliage will start to turn a dull gray color when it needs water. You can also check your footprints after you walk across the lawn. If the grass immediately pops back up, there is enough moisture in the leaf blades. But if the footprints remain compressed for a while, water your grass.

Water when you see one or both of these signs, but not before. Over-watering lawns results in shallow-rooted plants that are less tolerant of heat and drought, and more prone to disease. It also wastes water, money, and time.

Your soil texture, grass type, management style, rainfall, air and soil temperatures, wind, and humidity can all affect the amount and frequency of watering you will need to do.

How Much Water?

Water thoroughly but infrequently to grow healthy grass with deep roots. Light, frequent watering produces shallow, weak root systems that are more susceptible to heat and drought stress. Apply enough water to moisten the top 6 inches of soil. This provides an inch of water. Wait until the top 3 to 4 inches of soil are moist but crumbly, and then water again. Lawns growing in clay soils usually need a thorough watering once a week, while those in sandy soils need two applications (of half to three-fourths the needed water) each week. Water more frequently during extreme heat, or if you have drought-sensitive turf. Local water restrictions may dictate your watering schedule. More about conserving water is covered later in this chapter.

Over-watering can be just as harmful as not watering enough. Too much water leaches plant nutrients, especially nitrogen, past the root zone and even into the ground water. Watering too often results in waterlogged soils that limit root growth and increase the risk of disease.

It may take several hours of sprinkling to apply enough water to moisten the top 6 inches of soil. Don't just turn on the sprinkler and wait until you think you have applied enough. Check the setting and the time. Then use a soil probe or trowel to check the moisture. When the top 6 inches are moist, you know you have applied enough water. Note the sprinkler setting and time frame. Now you know how long it takes your sprinkler to apply the amount of water needed.

Measuring Irrigation
Water Output

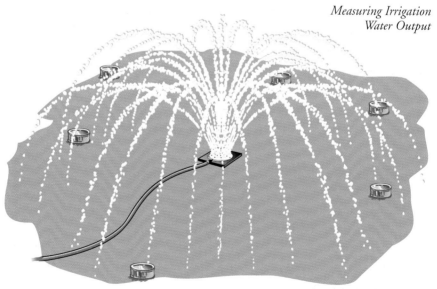

Or save yourself some digging and measure the water output. Place numerous shallow, straight-sided containers such as tuna cans randomly around the watering range of your irrigation system. Leave the system on for thirty minutes. Then measure the water in each container using a ruler, and figure the average depth in all the containers. If the system puts out an average of $^1/_2$ inch of water in thirty minutes, you know you need to leave it on for an hour to get an inch of water.

Sloped, compacted, or heavy soil may need special attention. Water often runs off the soil surface before it can penetrate and reach the grass roots. Apply a portion of the needed water, then move the sprinkler to another site. Come back later to apply the rest. Or set the timer on your sprinkler to water for several short periods.

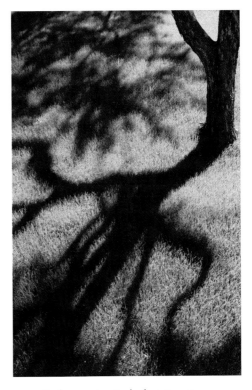

Early morning is the best time to water your lawn.

Aerate compacted soil to improve water penetration. Do this in spring or fall when the grass is actively growing—not in the heat of the summer when you are most likely to notice the problem. Guidelines on aeration are covered in Chapter Four.

When to Water

Early morning is the best time to water. An automatic timer comes in handy, allowing you to start the sprinklers without dragging yourself out of bed at the crack of dawn. Studies show water loss during early morning irrigation is 50 percent less than during the day or evening. There is also less risk of causing lawn diseases.

Irrigating after dew forms on turf (in the morning) typically does not increase the chance of disease. But irrigating before dew forms, such as in the

Investing in an automated irrigation system can pay for itself in a few years.

evening when you get home from work, prolongs the length of time the grass blades are wet, thus increasing the chances of disease problems. Watering grass in the heat of the day increases water loss due to evaporation.

Invest in an Irrigation System

Water-efficient irrigation designs and sprinkler heads are becoming more common. Rely on a professional, and get several estimates if you are not a do-it-yourself kind of gardener. If you are, however, you'll find plenty of good references and product guides to help you design and install your own irrigation system. Just remember that with lawns, especially, it is tempting to put in a few pulsating heads or ones with higher flow rates that cover a wide area. Systems that spray fine droplets of water across long distances are not the most efficient. Sprinklers that emit large drops of water closer to the ground are best. This type of system may require more sprinklers per site, but the money saved in water usage and by the plants using the water more efficiently will easily cover the cost of the system in the long run.

You can spread the cost of your irrigation system over several years if need be. Put in a few zones (small areas of the lawn) at a time, leaving connections for future expansion. Avoid poor designs that water the hardscape (driveways, sidewalks, and buildings) or that over-water trees, shrubs, and other plantings. Learn to adjust and reset your timers to allow for the age of the lawn and weather conditions since new lawns are watered differently than established ones. A rain sensor can help you avoid watering in the rain.

Preparing Your Lawn for Drought

The easiest way to deal with drought is to select a grass that is drought tolerant. Simple things like proper watering, raising the mowing height, mowing more frequently, and fertilizing properly will increase a lawn's tolerance to heat and drought.

The key to helping your grass survive or tolerate drought is to condition it so it doesn't need pampering. Remember that watering deeply and less often encourages deeper roots that are more drought tolerant. Gradually raising the mowing height 25 to 50 percent will also encourage deeper roots and help shade the soil. And by all means, keep the lawn mower blades sharp. Torn leaf blades increase moisture loss and stress to the plants.

Don't use fertilizer to compensate for a lack of water. Fertilizing is valuable to the growth and development of the grass plants but not during periods of drought and high soil and air temperatures. In fact, adding nitrogen can damage the lawn while increasing the vigor of heat-loving weeds.

Maintaining your entire lawn during times of severe water shortage is not always practical. If water rationing should occur, determine your lawn priority areas, watering just the high-traffic area, the portion of the lawn used for summer recreation, or the area closest to the house so it can help filter dust.

Of course, going dormant from drought is the natural way grass avoids stress. Lawns can remain dormant for two or three months and still recover. Your grass will turn brown, and weed seeds will sprout and thrive without competition from the grass. But once the temperature cools and rains return, a healthy lawn will recover.

Ways to Save Water

Select Drought-Tolerant Grass	Water Early in the Morning
Test and Amend Soil	Apply the Majority of Fertilizer
Add Organic Matter as	in Fall
Topdressing Whenever	Install a Water-Efficient
Possible	Irrigation System
Mow High	Avoid Runoff
Leave Grass Clippings on	Aerate Compacted Soils
the Lawn	

Fertilizing

Chapter Three

> **Apply Only What Is Needed**
> **Fertilize for Desired Maintenance Level**
> **Don't Fertilize When Lawn Is Wet**
> **Don't Fertilize When Lawn Is Stressed**
> **Split Rates in Half and Apply in Two Different Directions**
> **Water Summer Applications Thoroughly**
> **Be Careful with Weed-and-Feed Combinations**
> **Consider Organic and Slow-Release Products**

A little bit of nitrogen goes a long way in making your grass green and healthy. Overdoing it means more grass to cut, more thatch to control, and a greater risk of disease. Match your fertilizer program to the grass, soil, and your lawn care style, all of which affect the amount and timing of fertilizer applications.

Low-maintenance lawns are fertilized once each growing season, in late fall. Some people call this the lazy gardener's method; I prefer to call it low input. Lawns with a medium maintenance level can be fertilized two to three times each season, and those with a high level of maintenance are fertilized three to four times per season. Fertilization amounts and times are shown in the Introduction. Combine those with your soil test, the health of your lawn, and weather conditions to develop the schedule best suited for you and your lawn.

High-quality lawns with high use, such as athletic fields and golf courses, require the most maintenance. That means you mow, water, and dethatch more often to keep up the appearance. Residential lawns with average use can look good with a minimal or low level of care. You choose.

Sweet or Sour

Plant growth is affected by the soil acidity (sourness) and alkalinity (sweetness). The soil pH, a measure of acidity and alkalinity, influences the availability of soil nutrients for plant uptake. The pH scale ranges from 1 to 14, with 7 being neutral. Anything below 7 is acidic; anything above 7 is alkaline or basic. The scale is logarithmic, meaning that the distance from one number to the next is compounded. For example, a pH of 5 is ten times more acidic than a pH of 6 and one hundred times more acidic than a pH of 7.

This compounding difference may help you understand why a small numeric difference in pH can create significant differences in a plant's response. Certain plants grow well within only a narrow pH range, while others, less sensitive, tolerate a wider range. Changing the pH is also difficult due to the compounding difference. And many soils are highly buffered. This means that every time you try to change the pH, the soil tries to return to its previous state. It is much easier to grow plants and cultivars suited to your soil pH than to try to create a lasting change.

The slightly acidic pH of 6.5 is ideal for most plants. This is the pH level at which the nutrients needed by plants are most readily available. Turf prefers soil with a pH of 6.0 to 7.0, though I have seen it do quite well at higher pH levels. So let the grass, its health, and its appearance also be your guides.

Plant sensitivity to soil pH also depends on soil type and environmental conditions. Your soil test report provides pH levels and tells you how to adjust it, if needed, for the plants you are growing. Lime raises pH, while sulfur lowers pH. Always use your soil test as a guide since organic matter and

Changing Soil pH

Pounds of dolomitic or calcitic lime needed to raise pH to 6.5 in loam soil		Pounds of sulfur needed to lower the pH to 6.5 in loam soil	
Existing Soil pH	Pounds of Lime per 100 Sq. Ft.	Existing Soil pH	Pounds of Elemental Sulfur per 100 Sq. Ft.
6.0	3.5	8.5	4.8
5.5	7.5	8.0	3.6
5.0	10.0	7.5	2.4
		7.0	1.2

For best results have your soil tested and follow the recommendations for raising or lowering pH. The recommendations will be based upon the unique features of your soil. Soil texture and organic matter influence results. Never apply more than 15 pounds of lime per 100 square feet or 5 pounds of sulfur per 100 square feet in one season. Break large applications into smaller rates over a period of years.

soil texture must also be considered when amending the soil. The greater the organic matter in the soil, the more sulfur needed to lower the pH. The heavier the soil (more clay particles), the more lime and sulfur needed to change the pH. Never add more than 5 pounds of sulfur per 100 square feet or 15 pounds of lime per 100 square feet in one season. If larger amounts are needed, divide them into several smaller applications over two or more years. Or use acidifying fertilizers such as ammonium sulfate to help keep the soil surface acidic on high pH soils. It takes months, years, and even decades to change soil pH. So if you over-adjust the pH, it can take a long time to correct your mistake.

Essential Nutrients

There are sixteen nutrients or elements essential for proper plant growth. In turf care, we focus primarily on the major three—nitrogen (N), phosphorus (P), and potassium (K)—although the minor or secondary nutrients—calcium, magnesium, sulfur, iron, manganese, boron, molybdenum, copper, zinc, and chlorine—are also important. Carbon, hydrogen, and oxygen are non-mineral nutrients derived primarily from air and water.

Nitrogen produces healthy leaf and root growth, stimulates leaf color and density, and assists in resilience to stresses. Of course, the application timing and amount are important. Excessive nitrogen can encourage rapid leaf growth at the expense of root growth. It can also contribute to disease and insect infestation, thatch accumulation, and reduced heat and cold tolerance. Using higher rates of nitrogen can burn the turf and pollute waterways.

Phosphorus plays a critical role in establishing the root systems of lawn grasses. It is also helpful in energy transformation within the plant. Like nitrogen, excessive amounts of phosphorus can cause problems. Many lake communities have banned phosphorous-containing fertilizers that can end up in the lake and increase algal growth. Potassium is also associated with the health of the root system and is thought to play an even more vital role in the plant's ability to withstand environmental and mechanical stresses, including cold temperatures. Years of applying complete fertilizers, such as 10-10-10 or 12-12-12, have resulted in high levels of phosphorous and potassium in many soils. Have your soil tested, and follow those recommendations to avoid creating or increasing this problem.

Fertilize grass when it is actively growing. For cool-season grasses that means fertilizing between September and May, except during the coldest months, when the ground is frozen.

What to Feed

Your soil test report tells you what nutrients are needed and often recommends specific formulations that will accomplish the job. Select a fertilizer that best matches the soil test recommendations.

Because nitrogen moves through the soil quickly, it is hard to measure in the lab. Fertilizer recommendations for this nutrient are based on the average amounts of nitrogen used by grass plants growing in your type of soil. Additional nitrogen is needed each year to replace what is used by the plant. Grass clippings left on the lawn, topdressing with compost and composted manure, or adding chemical fertilizers will help keep your lawn healthy and attractive. Use the soil test recommendations as your starting point. Consider the health of your lawn, its growth rate, and the time and money you want to spend on your lawn's care in deciding how much nitrogen to use.

Test results may also indicate that phosphorus and potassium are needed. These products are relatively slow to move through the soil and take time to improve the health of your lawn. These two nutrients are usually incorporated into the soil before planting. Additional applications are not needed on a yearly basis, unless recommended by a soil test.

Good housekeeping applies to the outside of your house, as well as the indoors. Any product over-applied or spread haphazardly, with the excess left on the sidewalks and driveways, can wash into storm drains and water supplies. Fertilize sensibly and according to your lawn's needs and your soil test recommendations, not your best guess.

When to Feed

Let your grass tell you when to fertilize, just as it tells you when to water. Chlorotic yellow or dull green blades, as well as non-vigorous growth, may mean fertilizer is needed. But look at the whole picture before breaking out the spreader. Stress due to compacted soil—not lack of fertilizer—may be the problem, so adding fertilizer won't help. Improve drainage or other environmental stresses first so the plant can absorb and best use nutrients added later.

Rainfall and temperature also dictate when to fertilize. Drought-plagued lawns fed in the heat of the summer risk being burned and stressed unless regular irrigation can be provided. I find summer feedings help the weeds

Water your lawn after you have applied fertilizer, but not before. Applying fertilizer on wet grass can burn the foliage.

more than the grass. Always water the lawn after and not before feeding. Fertilizer tends to stick to wet leaves. Applying fertilizer when leaf blades are wet can burn or speckle the foliage, impacting the overall appearance of your lawn.

Cool-season grasses tend to grow best between September and May, so schedule feedings during these times except during the coldest months when the ground is frozen. That fertilizer ends up in the storm sewer or waterways, not in your lawn. Apply most (50 to 75 percent) of the recommended nitrogen in the fall. This encourages denser, not just taller, growth. Fertilizing outside the recommended months can stimulate unwanted weed growth and reduce grass hardiness.

Weed and Feed

Weed-and-feed products combine weed killer with fertilizer to eliminate the need for two separate applications. The idea is great for the applicator but not always best for the grass. Timing and rates of fertilizations and weed control do not always coincide. Besides, these products put weed killer on the lawn anywhere fertilizer is needed—the whole lawn. I prefer to spot-treat weeds or problem areas to minimize the use of chemicals and the impact on the environment.

Some gardeners use these products when their lawns are overrun with weeds or when they feel the convenience outweighs the downsides. Some weed-and-feed products, such as those that prevent crabgrass, contain a pre-emergent herbicide to prevent weed seeds from sprouting. These must be applied as the soil starts to warm, when it's about 50 degrees Fahrenheit. Use a thermometer to monitor soil temperatures or watch for the Vanhoutte spirea (bridal wreath spirea) to bloom. When the spirea is about to bloom, the soil is warm enough for crabgrass and other annual seeds to start sprouting. This is the best time to control crabgrass but not really the best time to fertilize.

Other weed-and-feed products contain broadleaf weed killers. These products kill existing weed plants. Apply these in spring or fall when the grass is actively growing and the temperatures are cool. Just as with the pre-emergents, you are sacrificing the best time for each of these operations and the option of spot-treating problems. Your lawn and the environment will benefit from using these products separately and at the proper time. As always, read and follow label directions carefully.

Organic Versus Synthetic

Contrary to popular belief, plants do not know the difference between organic fertilizers and manmade, synthetic fertilizers. Both are broken down by soil organisms into water-soluble materials available to the plants. I like organic products because of their slow-release action and benefits to the soil.

"Slow-release" means just that: the nitrogen is released slowly and made available to the plant over a longer period. Soil microbes, moisture, and temperature act on the fertilizer, breaking it down into a form the plant can use. Quick-release fertilizers dissolve easily in water and are immediately available to the plant. The unabsorbed portion of the fertilizer can be washed through the soil past the roots by excess rain and irrigation water.

Ammonium nitrate 33-0-0 is an example of a synthetic, laboratory-produced nitrogen fertilizer. Such inorganic fertilizers have both benefits and disadvantages. Advantages include quick availability to the plant and a quick response in growth and greening. Synthetic water-soluble fertilizers usually don't depend on temperature to work and are reasonably priced. I sometimes use these to supplement organic fertilizers in cool weather.

Disadvantages include a greater likelihood of loss from leaching caused by excess water, lowering of soil pH by fertilizers with ammonia, increase in pH due to lime carriers, high foliar burn potential, and a rapid surge in plant growth, requiring more mowing. Such products can be used more effectively by applying smaller amounts more often instead of applying the entire recommended amount at once. Or purchase a slow-release formulation that regulates the fertilizer's release of nitrogen. Some slow-release products include methylene urea, urea formaldehyde, sulfur-coated urea (SCU), polymer-coated urea (PCU), and isobutylidine diurea (IBDU).

Natural organic fertilizers include decayed living materials, manure, and bone meal (see Table 3.1 in the Appendix). The breakdown of these nutrients in the soil depends heavily on soil microorganisms. Natural organic fertilizers produce less foliar burn, very little leaching, and longer-lasting grass with more even growth. On the other hand, they typically have a low level of nutrients and require larger amounts to meet the plant's needs. They are slower to improve a plant's nutrient deficiency and do not break down as effectively in cooler temperatures. Other, even unpleasant, features can be objectionable odors, high phosphorus content compared to nitrogen, and the possible presence of salts, heavy metals, and weed seeds.

Winterizing Your Lawn

Some gardeners think fall fertilization is just a marketing ploy by garden centers to generate business at an otherwise slow time of year. But fall really is the best time to fertilize your lawn. The shorter days and cooler temperatures encourage root and stem growth. Fall fertilization promotes this type of growth without over-stimulating top growth. In the past, winterizing fertilizers were high in phosphorus (P) and potassium (K). It was thought they would promote a healthy root system and help the grass tolerate cold weather better. But it takes time for P and K to become available for the plant to use, so fall applications may not benefit the grass until later in the winter or even spring. Besides, most lawns already contain plenty if not excessive amounts of these nutrients. Applying more P and K when they aren't needed can harm the environment and certainly wastes time and money.

My recommendation is to rely on your soil test. If phosphorus and potassium are needed, then a fall application is fine unless you did one in the spring or the previous fall. If you routinely apply a complete fertilizer each spring, you do not need additional P and K in the fall. Consider using slow-release fertilizer. The grass will use what fertilizer is available in the fall, and the remaining nitrogen will be frozen in the soil. That nitrogen then will be available to the grass the following spring when the ground thaws and the soil warms. The slow release of this fertilizer helps the grass recover from winter without promoting excess top growth.

Reading a Fertilizer Bag

Fertilizers are sold based on the three main nutrients. The first number on the bag is nitrogen, the second number is phosphorus, and the third is potassium. For example, a bag of 10-20-10 has 10 percent of the total weight as nitrogen (NO_3 or NH_4), 20 percent phosphorus (P_2O_5), and 10 percent potassium (K_2O). The remaining weight to reach 100 percent could be secondary nutrients, such as iron, sulfur, and magnesium, and filler materials to bind the nutrients into a form that is easy to apply. A fertilizer containing all three nutrients is referred to as a "complete" fertilizer. Fertilizers with any nutrient missing, such as 45-0-0 or 13-0-44, are incomplete fertilizers.

Fertilizer analyses are also referred to by the ratio of nutrients. For example, 10-20-10 has a ratio of 1:2:1, 16-4-8 is 4:1:2, and 17-17-17 has a 1:1:1 ratio. If your soil test results suggest a fertilizer with a 3:1:2 ratio, you need a fertilizer similar to 12-4-8.

Each fertilizer bag must have a label clearly stating the ingredients of the contents. This statement shows the amount of each nutrient and its form. Slow-release, controlled-release, or water-insoluble forms of nitrogen are identified on the label, which also shows the percentage of the nutrient that is in slow-release form. Comparing the amounts of slow-release nitrogen to the price per pound of the fertilizer can help you make better buying decisions. Expect slow-release and properly sized and graded products to cost more but be well worth the investment.

Different levels of fertilizer maintenance will achieve different results, and require varying amounts of work. Choose a program that suits your lifestyle and expectations.

How Much to Apply

Fertilizer application rates are based on 1 pound of actual nitrogen per 1,000 square feet. For example, if you were using a complete fertilizer with an analysis of 13-13-13, the application rate would be 7.7 pounds of fertilizer per 1,000 square feet, since it contains only 13 percent actual nitrogen, not 100 percent. This was calculated by dividing 1 by 0.13, or dividing 100 by 13. This formula works no matter what the nitrogen, phosphorus, or potassium amount.

Another way to determine the amount to use and buy for your particular lawn is shown below.

100 divided by the percentage of nitrogen in the fertilizer times the square feet of lawn divided by 1,000 (standard application rate) = the amount of fertilizer needed to apply 1 pound of actual nitrogen to your lawn.

So if the analysis is 13-13-13 and you have a 2,000 square foot lawn, the formula is:

100 divided by 13 times 2,000 square feet divided by 1,000 square feet = 15.38 pounds of fertilizer

Many brands of fertilizer show on the bag the application rates that fall into the high-maintenance category and may be at a greater level than you want to apply. So calculating the rate based on the percentage of nitrogen in the fertilizer, your soil test results, and your maintenance level will allow you to apply the right amount of fertilizer for your lawn. It also will allow you to compare fertilizers based on nitrogen needs (see Table 3.2 in the Appendix).

Split the yearly fertilizer needs recommended by your soil test for medium- and high-maintenance lawns into several applications. See the fertilization chart in the Introduction for timing and rates.

How to Apply

With granular fertilizer, apply half the amount in one direction and the other half in the opposite direction to minimize skips and burns, similar to the seeding techniques discussed in Chapter One. There may still be some overlap and a few skips, but this is better than applying the fertilizer too heavily in one direction and causing dark green stripes in the lawn.

There are more scientific ways to apply fertilizer uniformly, but I have found that with smaller lawns, a hand-held broadcast applicator or seeder works nicely. I weigh the applicator empty, and then weigh it again after it is filled with the granular product, so I know how much I am applying based on my prefigured rate. For large lawns, drop and rotary spreaders are the norm.

Liquid fertilizer applied through hose-end applicators is also available and should be used in accordance with label directions. I find that most gardeners over-apply these products and burn the grass or under-apply and don't get the benefit from their effort. Liquid fertilizer N-P-K selections are very similar and may not match soil test recommendations, while granular types have a broader range of nutrient percentages to choose from and allow you to match soil deficiencies more closely. Applying phosphorus and potassium when they are not needed is a waste of money and may have adverse effects on the lawn and even on the environment.

Calibrating Fertilizer Spreaders

Brand-name spreaders will have instructions or settings for applying different rates of fertilizers. Some fertilizer bags even tell you the settings to use for particular kinds of spreaders. These settings should be checked periodically for accuracy.

Calibrate your fertilizer spreader to check these recommendations or to find the proper setting for your particular piece of equipment. The easiest way to calibrate a spreader is to fill the hopper with a pre-weighed amount of fertilizer to a noted level. Apply that amount over a pre-measured 1,000-square-foot area (20 feet × 50 feet). Weigh the amount left in the hopper, and subtract it from the initial amount. The initial amount weighed minus the amount left equals the amount applied per 1,000 square feet. Notice the setting or dial on the spreader to see whether it agrees with your calculations. If your spreader uses 5 pounds per 1,000 square feet, then you have a guide for future applications. You may need to adjust the control for the actual application to get the recommended amount. The calibration test also can be done using a 500-square-foot space. Just multiply the amount used by 2 to convert it to 1,000 square feet. Or calibrate over 100 square feet and multiply by 10.

The type of spreader and how fast you walk will have some bearing on the consistency of the amount applied. Drop spreaders cover smaller areas but are more uniform in application. Rotary spreaders cover more area but tend to throw the fertilizer more to one side.

You can also calibrate by applying fertilizer on a 20 × 50 (1,000 square foot) or 10 × 50 (500 square foot) plastic tarp. Any dimensions equaling 500 or 1,000 square feet will work. The fertilizer can then be collected and weighed. That way, you also will be able to see the throwing patterns of your particular spreader.

Or make this job even easier. Attach a collection hopper under the fertilizer dispenser. After walking the 1,000 square feet, weigh the fertilizer collected in the hopper. Calibrate as above. Once the settings are adjusted, return the fertilizer to the spreader and get going.

Many fertilizers and pH adjustment products are very dusty. Wearing gloves, a dust mask, and eye protection while applying them is strongly advised whether the product is synthetic or natural.

Fertilize your lawn wisely. Have your soil tested, carefully evaluate the health of your turf-grass, and take into account weather conditions before developing a fertilization schedule.

Mowing

> ### Mow Often
> ### Mow High
> ### Use Sharp Blades
> ### Mow in Alternating Patterns
> ### Recycle Clippings
> ### Invest in an Earth-Friendly Mower
> ### Consider a Mulching Mower or Blades
> ### Push, Don't Ride

The smell of fresh-cut grass and the rumble of a mower signal relaxation for some but just more work for others. No matter how you feel, it means stress for your lawn. Proper mowing can reduce stress—on you and the plants—while increasing the health and beauty of your lawn.

Mow Often

Most homeowners mow every seven to ten days. Most lawns in fact need to be cut every four to five days. It is best for the health and beauty of your lawn to follow the One-Third Rule: mow when the lawn gets one-third taller than the recommended growing height. For example, if you want to maintain your lawn at 2 inches, you should mow when the leaf blades reach 3 inches so that you remove only one-third of the blade at each mowing. That is all well and good, but unfortunately for those who mow every Saturday, no one told their grass to grow only one-third above its optimum height between mowings.

For my lawn, using the One-Third Rule means mowing every five days during the peak season even with minimal fertilization. It's impossible to always meet this schedule, but I find that more frequent mowings keep the lawn in the best shape. The smaller clippings fall easily into the grass, quickly breaking down with sunlight and moisture. So do the best you can to mow your lawn when needed, maintaining the One-Third Rule, and greener results will be just around the corner.

Spring rains, vacation, or too much other work can interfere with following the One-Third Rule. We often find ourselves "harvesting" the lawn, trying to quickly reduce the height of the overgrown grass. But a sudden reduction in the mowing height can traumatize your lawn. Changing the balance between the top growth and roots shocks the plant, halting root growth and thus weakening the overall health of the plant. So be kinder to your lawn and correct the problem over time. Gradually reduce the cutting height over several mowings until the recommended height is achieved.

Keep mowing as long as the grass is growing. Avoid mowing wet grass: it causes clippings to clump and you to slip and fall. The hot, dry weather of summer means that you and the grass start to slow down. Continue the One-Third Rule, but decrease mowing frequency to every seven to ten days. Don't mow dormant lawns; there's no need. Just try to keep the weeds cut (though not by mowing) so they don't go to seed. And enjoy the reprieve. As the rains return and the weather cools, you'll be mowing more often. During mild falls when the grass keeps growing and I keep mowing, I remember that a snow shovel is my alternative. In that context, mowing seems less of a burden.

Mow, Then Measure

It's a good idea to measure the actual length of the leaf blade after you mow to determine exactly how the height compares to the mower deck setting you're using. Most mowers have mechanisms that allow adjustments

Mowing grass high encourages deeper root systems, which are better able to withstand environmental stresses.

to raise or lower the body of the mower. Instead of just depending on guesswork to find the correct setting, take a ruler and measure the height of the grass blades in several locations immediately after mowing. The ground level varies across your lawn, so an average of these measurements will give you a better idea of the height at which each setting really cuts. First, measure the mower setting on a sidewalk or driveway. Then check the mowing height by measuring the grass. Now adjust the mower setting to achieve the desired height.

Mow High

One common misconception is that the shorter you cut the lawn, the slower it will grow, so you won't have to mow as often. If you keep cutting the grass so short that you are almost scalping it, you may not have to mow as often because it will likely die. Shorter grass produces shallow roots and is less tolerant of heat and drought. It also allows more sunlight to reach the soil surface, which encourages more weed seeds to germinate. As the grass declines, the weeds begin to take over—and you will have to mow these unwanted plants even more often than your grass. Taller grass also filters pollutants better and serves as a living mulch for the lawn, minimizing soil temperatures and reflective heat.

Grass roots generally mirror the grass blades, so the taller the grass, the deeper the roots. This is what you want, since deep roots make the grass more resistant to drought, heat, cold, and pests. Keep Midwest lawns at least $2^1/2$ to $3^1/2$ inches tall. Cut the lawn whenever the grass is $3^1/2$ to 4 inches tall. Raise the mowing height whenever the grass is stressed from heat, drought, or shade. There is no need to reduce the mowing height in the fall.

Sharp Blades Are Better

Have you changed your lawn mower blades lately? Dull blades chew, rip, or tear grass. So if you haven't sharpened or replaced your blades and think you are mowing at a particular height, you are fooling yourself. Torn grass blades often die back to below the tear, making the blade shorter than the original cut. Shredded grass blades are also more likely to succumb to disease and are more susceptible to heat and drought stress. Sharp mower blades also save on fuel consumption. According to one study, mowing with sharp blades can reduce fuel use by as much as 20 percent.

Rotary vs. Reel Mowers

Rotary	Reel
Initial low cost	Low yearly cost (no gas or oil)
Easy to maneuver	Quiet
Basic maintenance	Only maintenance is sharpening blades
Ideal for uneven surfaces	Smooth cut (better on level ground)
No raking (with mulching mowers)	No emissions

Sharp mower blades give a clean, smooth cut. They also make the mowing process more efficient, causing less stress on both the mower and the grass. The easiest way to keep blades sharp is to buy an extra set and switch blades several times a season. This is a minimal investment that pays big dividends in the health of your lawn. Disconnect the spark plug wire when

Vary your mowing patterns in order to prevent soil compaction. If you mow in one direction one week, then mow perpendicular or diagonal to that the next week.

changing the mower blades. A "C" clamp, available at any hardware store, can keep the blades from turning while you are loosening and tightening the bolts. There is even a Blade Buster™ tool made especially for this purpose. The worst thing to do is try holding the blades, with or without gloves, dull or not, with your hands. These tools or something similar can help prevent serious cuts to your hands and fingers.

Don't Be Set in Your Ways

Soil compaction occurs over time, usually from the weight of mowing or gardening equipment, pet runs, or frequent foot traffic. Areas near sidewalks and pathways are likely to become compacted first. Soil type also plays a role. Clay soils are more likely to compact than sandy, silty, or loamy soil. Soil compaction causes problems such as poor root growth, poor oxygen penetration to the roots, and poor water filtration, all of which mean poor plant performance. One of the biggest contributions to soil compaction in your lawn is mowing in the same direction week after week, year after year. It is easy to change directions every time you mow. If you first mow in a perpendicular direction, then the next time in a diagonal one, you can go at least four different ways, spreading the path of the lawnmower tires over a larger surface area. You'll also be surprised at how different the view looks when you vary the direction of your mowing. You may become quite the "lawn artist."

To Bag or Not to Bag?

A 1,000-square-foot lawn can generate 200 pounds or more of clippings annually. The clippings contain about 4 percent nitrogen (N), 2 percent phosphorus (P), and 0.5 percent potassium (K). Leaving clippings on the lawn can add as much as 1 pound of nitrogen per 1,000 square feet each season. So it doesn't make sense to pay to fertilize the lawn, then cut the grass and throw away part of the fertilizer. Frequent mowing, minimal feedings, and proper watering allow you to leave the clippings and benefit the lawn at the same time. If you leave the clippings on the lawn, you can reduce your fertilizer needs by as much as 25 percent over a five to seven year period.

On the other hand, leaving thick clumps of grass on the lawn after mowing can be detrimental, causing the grass underneath to yellow, brown, and possibly die. This practice also encourages disease and mold and can contribute to thatch problems, especially if large quantities are left on a regular basis. If rain, vacation, or other causes keep you from mowing and result in long clippings, use a mulching mower or rake to remove those clippings.

Mulching mowers and mulching blades cut grass into smaller pieces, which helps eliminate the need for bagging or removing lawn clippings. Mulching mowers take less time than bagging, since you don't have to stop to empty a bag every few rounds. But bagging certainly is easier than raking and removing by hand. Mulching mowers must be pushed or driven more slowly than other mowers to allow time for the clippings to be chopped up properly. If you don't have a mulching mower, try making a second pass over the cut lawn. Use a higher setting to help cut and disperse clippings so they will decay quickly. Of course, the effectiveness of all these methods depends on the amount of accumulated clippings.

Many municipalities limit or even prohibit grass clippings from landfills to avoid filling them with a valuable and reusable resource. Recycling the clippings as mulch in the garden or an ingredient in the compost pile is a good way to recycle the moisture and nutrients back into your landscape. But be careful how you manage clippings collected from a lawn recently treated with an herbicide (weed killer). The pesticide can leach from the clippings into the soil and damage your plants. It is best to leave treated clippings on the lawn. Or thoroughly compost them before use. Mix the clippings with dried leaves or compost, turn them frequently, and wait until the green debris turns to rich compost. Some chemicals such as clopyralid persist and should not be used in compost piles.

Thatch—The Real Story

Thatch is a layer of partially decayed grass located between the soil and the leaf blades of the turf plants. It is composed primarily of roots, rhizomes, and stolons, not grass clippings. Thatch formation is a routine part of the growth cycle, in which plant parts age, die, and decompose into humus. The problem occurs when something upsets this natural cycle, causing thatch to build up more quickly than it can break down. Rapid, excessive lawn growth is the major cause of thatch, and over-fertilization and over-watering are the biggest culprits. They produce excessive growth and long clippings, preventing the normal breakdown of thatch.

A thin layer of thatch, less than $1/2$ inch, is actually good for the lawn. It acts as a cushion to minimize compaction and wear. It also mulches the ground, helping conserve moisture. The problem arises when the thatch layer exceeds $1/2$ inch. This thicker layer prevents water and fertilizer from reaching the soil, harbors insects and diseases, and leads to shallow root systems that are more susceptible to cold, heat, and drought stress.

Monitor your lawn, checking at least once a season for thatch problems. If the ground feels spongy and soft as you walk across it, you may have a thatch problem. Check these and other areas throughout the lawn. Use a knife to cut through the grass and thatch and into the soil. Remove pie-shaped wedges from several areas throughout the lawn. An average of $1/2$ inch or more thatch on these samples means it is time to get to work and reduce this layer.

Grass with
Thatch Layer

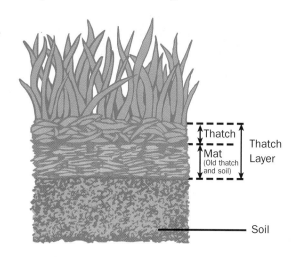

There are several ways to deal with thatch. Vertical mowers and dethatching equipment, which can be rented from tool centers or home centers, mechanically reduce the thatch layer. They have blades, knives, or tines that lift the dead vegetation to the surface where it can be raked, then composted. You can also use a hand-rake to pull thatch to the surface, but doing so is time-consuming, strenuous work, and most people don't do it vigorously enough to deal with severe thatch buildup. Dethatching is stressful on the lawn, not very effective, and should be done only in spring or fall when the grass is actively growing. Brace yourself for the aftermath. A freshly dethatched lawn is thin, sparse, and quite unattractive. Take advantage of this by overseeding the lawn to promote thicker, healthier growth.

Core aeration is the other mechanical means of reducing thatch. This process also helps reduce soil compaction, so you get two benefits from one operation. Aerate the lawn in spring or fall when the grass is actively growing. Core aerators remove plugs of grass, thatch, and soil, allowing air, water, and nutrients to reach the roots. This mimics earthworm activity by helping the thatch layer to decompose. Use a machine that grinds the cores and spreads them over the soil surface. If this isn't possible, grind the cores yourself using your rotary mower. Just be sure to replace or sharpen the blades when you are done.

In severe thatch cases, spread your removal efforts over two or three years rather than relying on a single operation. This will minimize stress to the lawn and invite fewer weed problems. Adequate soil moisture also makes the process much easier and less stressful to the lawn.

Recommended Rates for Topdressing per 1,000 Square Feet of Lawn Area:		
Topdressing Thickness *(Inches)*	*Cubic Volume* *(Cubic Feet)*	*(Cubic Yards)*
$1/8$	10.42	0.39
$1/4$	20.83	0.77
$5/16$	26.04	0.96
$3/8$	31.25	1.16
$1/2$	41.67	1.54
$5/8$	52.08	1.93
$3/4$	62.50	2.31
1	83.30	3.09

Topdressing

Topdressing helps reduce thatch and smoothes or levels the soil. This technique involves spreading a thin layer of topsoil, compost, peat moss, or other organic material over the soil surface. The topdressing material comes in contact with the thatch, adding soil microorganisms that help break it down. Topdress and core aerate at the same time for best results. Ideally, the topdressing material should be similar to the existing soil. Applying highly organic products or sand that form distinct layers can encourage shallow roots. Suggested topdressing rates vary, but $1/2$ to 2 cubic yards of material per 1,000 square feet will produce a layer that is $1/8$ to $5/8$ inch thick. If you are topdressing with heavy amounts, use multiple, light applications throughout the growing season. Drag, rake, or brush the topdressing material so it makes good contact with the ground surface. This is also a good time to fill in low spots and overseed thin lawns. You may want to rent a topsoil spreader or hire a professional for large jobs. Water thoroughly and fertilize as needed to help your lawn recover.

Getting Ready for Winter

Keep cutting the grass as long as it continues to grow. Follow the One-Third Rule; fortunately, your grass will be putting on more root and horizontal growth and less height. This means less frequent mowing. Maintain the tall recommended mowing height throughout the fall. There is no need to reduce the mowing height for winter. Taller grass means deeper roots and more cold tolerance.

Do remove leaves from the grass. I prefer to shred mine with the mower and leave them on the lawn. Mulching mowers can do this with one pass. You may need to run your non-mulching mowers over the lawn several times to chop the leaves into finer pieces. These small pieces drop to the ground, adding organic matter and nutrients to the soil. No matter how you cut it, as long as you can see the grass through the leaf pieces, you won't harm your lawn. In fact, you're doing two chores in one: improving the soil while managing autumn leaves.

Or recycle this valuable resource and use it for composting and soil improvement. Many gardeners bag their leaves and add them to the compost pile. This can be tedious and involve lots of hauling, so consider using your mower and a circular mowing pattern to make this job easier. Mow in a continuous diminishing circle headed in the same direction, blowing the leaves into the center. By the time you reach the center, you have a narrow pile of shredded leaves. Rake and use these in the compost pile or till them into annual vegetable and flower gardens for soil improvement. Never leave full-sized leaves on the lawn. They eventually pack down and smother the plants. The lack of light and moisture trapped around the crown of the plants leads to disease and even plant death. And you know what moves in to these dead spots in the spring—weeds!

Protect the Environment and Get in Shape

If it is gasoline-powered, your mowing equipment impacts the environment through smog-forming emissions such as carbon monoxide and nitrogen oxide. Mowers manufactured after 1997 run 70 percent cleaner than earlier models. According to the Outdoor Power Equipment Institute, less than

Wise Mower Maintenance

Change oil seasonally

Recycle oil

Replace spark plug and air filter seasonally

Fill the gasoline tank only three-quarters full,

allowing for heat expansion

Avoid gasoline spills

Keep blades sharp and decks clean of clippings

Review owner's manual

2 percent of smog-forming emissions come from today's lawn and garden equipment. Walk-behind, as opposed to riding, mowers contribute even smaller amounts, estimated at less than 1 percent. Other alternatives are cordless electric or rechargeable battery-operated mowers. There are also improved reel mowers that weigh only 16 to 31 pounds (much better than the 40- to 60-pound models from years ago!) and are ideal for small lawns of $1/2$ acre or less.

Helping the environment can also be good for your health. Did you know that when you push instead of ride, you expend as much as 450 calories per hour, which is about the same as when playing tennis or cycling? Push mowing also improves your upper-body tone and cardiovascular conditioning. Mowing the lawn or working in your garden 45 minutes each day can lower your heart attack risk to one-third that of non-exercisers. So mow your way to a healthier body and lawn!

End of Season Care for Power Mowers

Run engine until all fuel is gone

While engine is warm, drain oil and replace with fresh oil

Clean deck

Lubricate appropriate parts

Remove battery and charge it before storage

Enjoy the break from mowing!

Low Maintenance Lawn Ideas

Chapter Five

Lawnscaping—Wise Use of Turf

Divide and Conquer

Curves, Not Corners

Create Islands of Plants in a Sea of Grass

Narrow Strips of Grass—Too Much Work

Edging and Mowing Strips

High Traffic Areas

Shade-Tolerant Alternatives

Moss—Weed or Garden Plant

Lawnscaping

Proper care will keep your lawn healthy and attractive, but proper planning can help you get the most value for the least amount of work. Our landscapes usually start out as a sea of green, and we gradually add a few trees, a hedge, and maybe a flower garden or two. Soon that green sea of grass is nothing but tiny islands that are difficult to mow and not too attractive. Give your lawn the same amount of consideration you give your trees, shrubs, and flowers. After all, grasses are plants—in fact, there are 850 of them per square foot and 8.5 million in a 10,000-square-foot area.

It takes careful planning to place and grow that many plants in one yard. "Lawnscaping" or "turfscaping," a fancy name for the wise use and placement of turf, does just that. It takes a look at the best way to use grass to meet your needs while reducing maintenance. Avoid growing grass in narrow strips or other areas the mower won't fit or can't reach. Consider using ground covers or shrubs on steep slopes that are difficult and dangerous to mow. Look at alternative plants or hardscape materials for areas along walkways and drives where grass dies from compaction, de-icing salt, and foot traffic. All this will give you a good-looking lawn and landscape with much less effort. And I'm all for low-input lawn care.

Creating curved edges on your landscape beds makes for easier and quicker mowing.

Divide and Conquer

If you are fortunate enough (or maybe unfortunate enough, depending on your view) to have a large yard, you probably have lots of grass. This may mean weekends spent cutting, raking, and managing that huge expanse of green. If this is not your idea of fun, consider replacing some of the grass with planting beds or prairie. Your remaining beautiful green lawn will make these areas stand out and be noticed.

Start by quickly sketching the overall design of your existing yard. Does it meet your family's needs in terms of recreation, entertainment, and beauty? Note any adjustment to the landscape that needs to be made. Now take a look from inside out. What views do you need to screen? Which ones do you want to keep? Screening requires that you plant something taller than grass, such as trees and shrubs. Perhaps you want a flower garden or water feature outside your kitchen window. Many gardeners plant prairies beyond their lawn area. They still have green grass near the house but enjoy a beautiful low-maintenance prairie at the back of their property. Jot down your desires and ideas on your landscape sketch. Make sure the lawn areas are part of the planning process, not just an afterthought. Next, prioritize the list and start tackling these projects one at a time, continuously evaluating your landscape design.

Curves, Not Corners

Use flowing lines, not corners, when designing new beds or redesigning existing planting areas. Gentle curves are pleasing to the eye and much easier and less time-consuming to mow around. Design or replace landscape bed corners with long sweeping curves. Curves eliminate the need to stop, back up, and struggle to reach all the grass with the mower. You'll also save time spent hand-trimming those few grass blades the mower just can't reach. Use a garden hose or rope to design the layout of your beds. Lay the hose or rope on the ground and move it around until you create the design you like. Avoid drastic curves; they can be as difficult to maneuver around as corners. Now drive or push your mower, engine off, around the edge of the bed. Make any adjustments necessary to create an easy mowing pattern.

Create Islands of Plants in a Sea of Grass

Evaluate your existing plants and future plans. Consider growing trees, shrubs, and flowers in beds. This community-style planting is better for the plants and easier to mow around. Grass competes with trees for water and nutrients. Studies have shown that young trees are often stunted when grass is allowed to grow right up to the trunk. Even older trees can be affected. I observed this at the campus where I teach. We had a fifteen-year-old catalpa tree so pathetic that my students called it a shrub. Then the grounds staff increased the size of the mulch bed around the tree. The next season the tree doubled its normal growth rate. Eight years later, it finally looks like a tree instead of a shrub on steroids.

Group trees together or mix them with other plants. Mulch the large beds to help keep down weeds. Do not use weed barrier fabric under woodchips and other organic mulches. Plant ground covers and perennials to help soften the mulch and unify the planting. Or create beds around existing trees. Design large planting beds that include several existing trees and shrubs. Kill the grass and mulch the area. Now you will be mowing around one large garden instead of several individual trees and shrubs.

Eliminating the grass growing next to the tree eliminates one of the biggest tree killers—mower blight. This problem starts when gardeners damage the tree trunk by using their mowers and weed whips next to the trunk trying to get every last blade of grass. The nicks and cuts made by this equipment create wounds that are perfect entryways for insects and disease. Mower-blighted trees are easy to spot: they are the first to show signs of damage during drought and other stressful periods. Creating planting beds keeps mowers and weed whips at a safe distance from the trunks of trees and stems of shrubs. Best of all, it saves you time and effort. Instead of cutting around individual plants, you are cutting around large islands. If you include a mowing strip, described later in this chapter, you will also eliminate the need to hand trim.

Narrow Sections of Turf—Too Much Work

Avoid creating narrow strips of grass between the sidewalk and curb or planting beds. These areas are difficult to reach with a mower and weed-eater. It often takes more time and effort to get the mower to the grass than to mow the strip. The lighter weight weed-eaters are more maneuverable, but all too often, they accidentally cut down nearby flowers. Grass along walks and roads is subject to high concentrations of de-icing salts. This means you have to replace dead grass along walks, drives, and roadways each spring. Consider installing hardscapes with curb designs that keep out salt or a buffer edge of pavers where the salt-laden water can drain. Or use a low-maintenance and stress-tolerant ground cover in place of grass. This gives you a green look without the mowing. Select a ground cover that not only tolerates the conditions but also complements your other plantings.

Edging or Mowing Strips

Grass always seems to grow where we don't want it—in the flower bed. Many gardeners use plastic or steel edging to keep the grass out of flower gardens, shrub beds, and tree plantings. Select a material that won't be heaved out of the ground by frost during our harsh winters. Or skip the edging material, and just use a shovel or edger to physically dig an edge around each bed.

Mowing Strips Along Landscape Beds

Edging keeps the grass out of the beds but requires that you hand-trim the nearby grass. This is often the last task I get around to. I always have the best of intentions, but on my way to get the clippers, I get sidetracked by a weed that needs pulling or a flower that needs deadheading. Those grassy stragglers left by the mower are quickly for-gotten and left to grow for several weeks. When I finally can't stand it, I get out the grass clippers—though by then a machete would be more appropriate—and cut the stragglers back. Avoid the hassle, reduce your work, and keep your gardens and lawn looking good by creating mowing strips around each bed.

Mowing strips can be as fancy as pavers or as natural as woodchips. The idea is to create an edge around each bed to keep the grass out of the flowers and to create a flat surface for the mower tires. This allows you to cut the grass right up to the bed edge without damaging your flowers—and without hand-trimming.

Mowing strips also work around raised beds. We used this technique when designing our Harvest 4 the Hungry garden. A local stone company donated the materials, and the Wisconsin Landscape Contractors Association installed them around our raised beds. This made mowing much easier for the grounds manager who had to cut the grass around the raised beds.

At home, our landscape has a more informal look. We use a shovel to edge the beds, creating a shallow trench. We fill the trench with woodchips to create a level edge for the mower tires. The trench keeps the grass out of the beds and eliminates the need to trim the grass by hand. And the few chips that accidentally fly into the grass are easily raked back in place.

Reduce cleanup of grass clippings by aiming the mower's discharge away from the garden. Nothing is more unsightly or discouraging than to see your nicely manicured flower bed or clean sidewalks and drive showered with fresh clippings. Keeping the clippings on the lawn saves cleanup time and keeps this valuable resource, clippings, on the lawn where it belongs.

High-Traffic Sites

Grass is meant for walking and play, but too much foot traffic can damage the lawn. You can probably trace your dog's run, the kids' shortcut to their friends, and the area of your lawn used for the neighborhood ball game. This constant wear and tear can damage even the toughest lawn. Replace or overseed large areas with more wear-tolerant grasses. Look for cul-tivars and grass mixes labeled as wear resistant or tolerant of high traffic. Tall fescue is a coarse grass often used in playing fields and other high-traffic areas. Supina bluegrass is a good choice for moist, shady areas that receive a lot of use. But it is very expensive and hard to find. If this doesn't work, you may need to look for alternatives.

The Ohio State University campus has the perfect example: the Oval. As an undergraduate, I was told the crisscross sidewalks were built after years of students wearing shortcuts in the grass as they walked between the buildings. Whether built to contain student traffic or after the fact, the walkways have saved the rest of the grass from the wear of thousands of students traversing the Oval to get to class.

Consider replacing the worn turf in your lawn with a brick, concrete, woodchip, or other decorative and functional walkway. Select a material that complements the rest of your landscape and a surface that fits your needs.

Dead Nettle

Ajuga

Perennial ground covers can be used instead of turfgrass. Some good choices are ajuga, thyme, sweet woodruff, Canadian ginger, hosta, and dead nettle.

Thyme

The walkway should be safe to use in all types of weather and should allow you to move equipment, such as wheelbarrows, across it easily. If the path needs to be cleared in winter, select an easy-to-shovel surface. Try a combination of plants and hardscape if you want to maintain the green in your walkway. A longtime favorite is thyme planted between flagstone steppers. This combination makes an attractive and fragrant walkway as your feet brush over the plants. Or use some of the new plastic and block drive and walkway products that create a supportive surface while allowing grass to grow through the open spaces.

Shade-Tolerant Alternatives

Every new landscape and lawn comes with a few trees. As the trees grow and mature, they block cold winter winds, cool the house in summer— and shade out your sun-loving grass. This frustrates many homeowners who spend every summer and lots of money trying to grow a lawn in the dense shade of a Norway maple or other shade tree. The tree always wins. So stop fighting a hopeless battle and look for reasonable alternatives.

Try growing a shade-tolerant grass mix, not just shade-tolerant Kentucky bluegrass. Though more tolerant than the standard bluegrass, shade-tolerant cultivars are not as good in shade as fine fescue, rough bluegrass, and supina bluegrass. Use a grass seed mixture containing at least 50 percent fine fescue for dry, shaded areas. Water shaded lawns deeply, moistening the top 3 to 4 inches of soil, but less frequently than lawns growing in full sun. Wait until the grass turns a bluish green, shows signs of wilt, or shows footprints when walked upon. Since the plants receive less light and water, they need less fertilizer. Over-fertilizing can lead to poor root development. Fertilize shade lawns at the same time as sun lawns, but use half the amount.

If shade grass mixes don't work, or you are looking for something other than grass, try a shade-tolerant ground cover. Lamium (dead nettle), pachysandra, and Canadian ginger are just a few of the ground covers that grow in shaded areas inhospitable to turf. See the Appendix for a list of a few of the shade-tolerant ground covers.

Mulch is a first choice for some gardeners and a last resort for others. For me, it is a first choice. Woodchip mulch and shredded bark keep weeds at bay, conserve moisture, and generally improve the trees' environment. I like the natural look of mulch under my trees. Many gardeners don't like woodchips in their landscape, but woodchips definitely beat bare soil, weeds, or the unsightly mess that results under the dense shade of some trees.

Or try to increase the light reaching the grass by thinning out the crowns of your trees. Consult a certified arborist for best results. Tree-care professionals can safely and properly remove some branches to allow more light to reach the grass below. It is worth the money to hire a knowledgeable professional who will do the job right. Improper pruning can weaken the tree and ruin its beauty. You can have both grass and trees in your landscape with proper design and management strategies.

Create a Moss Garden

Moss garden? You may think I'm nuts if you are one of the gardeners struggling to kill the moss so you can grow grass. In that case, see Chapter Seven for tips on eliminating this weed. If you are tired of fighting the moss, you may want to add a few flagstones and call it a garden. Moss gardens have become quite trendy, and articles abound with tips on growing this plant that many gardeners have tried to kill.

As with any garden plant, you need to understand moss and its preferred growing conditions to have a successful moss garden. Moss prefers moist shady conditions. It will fill in bare areas caused by soil compaction, poor drainage, or acidic soils. Take advantage of this, and start your moss garden where it likes to grow. This is usually under a tree or next to the north side of the house. The presence of moss is the first sign that you've picked the right location.

Mosses have no true roots, flowers, fruit, or seed. They spread by spores or by sending out new shoots. Keep this in mind as you encourage the moss to grow and spread. Try collecting small pieces of moss and mixing them with water. Wait a few minutes. Or better yet, mix them in a blender (ask the cook first) and create a moss slurry. Spray or paint the watery moss solution on the bare areas, then wait. Soon you will see your moss garden grow and spread before your eyes. Or expand the garden by placing pieces of existing moss in nearby bare spots. Make sure the moss fully contacts the soil. Anchor it in place with a nail, wire, or stake until it attaches to the soil. Keep the moss well watered but not soggy. Fall or spring, when the weather is cool and moist, are the best times to establish moss. Be patient. It may take five weeks before you see any signs of new growth.

Turf Varieties

Chapter Six

> *Cool-Season Grass Mixes*
>
> *Match Grass to the Growing Area and Soil Type*
>
> *Consider Personal Preferences*
>
> *Evaluate Maintenance Requirements*
>
> *Research Varieties and Their Availabilities*
>
> *Use the Most Pest-Resistant Cultivars Available*
>
> *Selection of Grasses*

Growing healthy and attractive plants begins with selecting the right plant for the growing conditions. The same holds true for your lawn. The selection is a little more limited since only cool-season grasses are an option in the Midwest, but the numerous varieties help provide many alternatives to meet the growing conditions in your yard.

The main grass of the Midwest is bluegrass. Its fine texture and rich green have made it a favorite of lawn lovers for many years. Some cultivars tolerate shade better than others. This cool-season grass prefers full sun and well-drained soil but will tolerate light shade. It goes dormant during hot, dry weather but most varieties recover from drought once moisture and cool temperatures return. While bluegrass withstands the normal wear of a home lawn, it can show signs of stress when the lawn becomes an athletic field for the neighborhood children.

Fine fescue, including hard, creeping red, and chewings, is the other major grass of the Midwest. "Fine" is a good term for this extremely narrow-leafed grass. Much more shade tolerant than bluegrass, it allows lawn lovers to grow a carpet of green in both the sunny and shady portions of the yard. Cultivars have been selected to blend with the texture and color of bluegrass, while maintaining their shade and drought tolerance. Fine fescues are slow to spread and less tolerant than bluegrass of the normal wear of a home lawn, but some cultivars have been selected for their increased durability.

Cool-Season Turfgrass Comparisons

Characteristics*	Kentucky Bluegrass	Creeping Red Fescue	Chewings Fescue	Hard Fescue
Growing Height	2$^1/_2$ to 3$^1/_2$	2 to 4	2 to 4	2 to 3$^1/_2$
Growth Habit	Spreading	Weakly Spreading	Bunch	Bunch
Color	Deep Green	Deep Green	Deep Green	Deep Green
Texture	Fine	Extremely Fine	Extremely Fine	Extremely Fine
Preferred Soil pH **	6.0 to 7.0	5.5 to 7.0	5.5 to 7.0	5.5 to 7.0
Shade Tolerance	Poor	Excellent (dry)	Excellent (dry)	Excellent (dry)
Drought Tolerance	Poor	Good	Good	Good
Heat Tolerance	Poor	Fair	Fair plus	Fair
Cold Tolerance	Excellent	Excellent	Excellent	Excellent
Hardiness Zones	3	3	3	3
Wearability	Moderate	Fair	Fair	Fair
Salt Tolerance	Poor	Poor	Poor	Poor

Characteristics*	Perennial Ryegrass	Rough Bluegrass	Supina Bluegrass	Tall Fescue
Growing Height	2 to 3$^1/_2$	$^1/_2$ to 2	1 to 2	2$^1/_2$ to 3$^1/_2$
Growth Habit	Bunch	Spreading Stolon	Spreading Stolon	Bunch
Color	Deep Green	Apple Green	Yellow Green	Medium Green
Texture	Medium	Fine	Fine	Medium to Coarse
Preferred Soil pH **	6.0 to 7.0	6.0 to 7.0	6.0 to 7.0	5.0 to 8.5
Shade Tolerance	Fair (moist)	Good to Excellent (moist)	Good to Excellent (moist)	Good
Drought Tolerance	Poor	Poor	Poor	Good
Heat Tolerance	Fair	Fair	Fair	Good
Cold Tolerance	Poor	Excellent	Good	Good
Hardiness	3***	3	3	4
Wearability	Good	Fair	High	Good
Salt Tolerance	Fair	Poor		Fair

*Variations exist between cultivars within each species.

** Turgrass can tolerate pH outside this range. Let your soil test and the health and appearance of your grass be your guide.

***Perennial ryegrass can be short lived in the far north regions of the Midwest.

Ryegrass completes the big three Midwest grasses. This grass makes up a portion of most grass seed mixes. It is fast sprouting, provides quick cover, and serves as a living mulch for the slower growing bluegrass and fescue. Annual rye was the choice of the past. It was functional, short lived (one year), and unattractive. Perennial rye has taken over as the choice for lawn mixes.

The turf-type ryegrasses blend better with fescue and bluegrass than the annual species does. Newer varieties are quicker to establish, helping keep aggressive weeds at bay until the bluegrass and fescue become established and create a dense lawn. Perennial ryegrass is often promoted as a tough grass for use in high-traffic areas. But you should avoid using high-traffic mixes with a high percentage of perennial rye unless they can be regularly over-seeded. Not reliably hardy or long lived in the far north, perennial rye is best used as a temporary part of those Midwest lawns. Do not use any lawn seed mix that contains more than 15 to 25 percent ryegrass unless you want a mostly ryegrass lawn. Most grass seed mixes are a blend of bluegrass, fine fescue, and perennial ryegrass unless you want a mostly ryegrass lawn. The ideal percentage of each varies with the growing conditions and intended use of the lawn. Grass mixes intended for sunny yards contain anywhere from 50 to 100 percent bluegrass. Since most lawns are a mix of sun and shade, a seed mix containing 55 to 75 percent bluegrass, 25 to 35 percent fescue, and the remainder perennial ryegrass works well. Shade mixes should be at least 55 percent fescue, less than 25 percent bluegrass, and no more than 15 percent ryegrass.

The information on the specific types of turfgrasses on the following pages is organized in order of their importance and frequency of use in Midwest lawns.

Low-Maintenance Lawn Mix

Many homeowners would like a nice-looking lawn without much mowing and fertilizing. It is possible to have healthy green grass with minimal care. But be aware that the "look" is quite different between highly managed turf and a low-maintenance lawn. I find the difference acceptable, but other gardeners—or your neighbors—may not. Moreover, the taller, less-managed grass is more susceptible to weeds and voles and more difficult to run through and play upon. So before you change your ways, make sure you will end up with the results you and your family desire.

Most seed mixes sold as low maintenance contain 100 percent fine fescue. These lawns can be left unmowed. The grass will grow 2 feet tall, bend gracefully, and put on a flower display. You will have to remove noxious weeds and woody plants that invade the grass. Fertilize once or twice a year depending on the health and vigor of the grass and your soil type. Remove leaves in the fall. Rake or mow the leaves, allowing small pieces of leaves and short clippings to remain on the lawn.

A slightly more conservative approach requires just a bit more care. For best results, use a mix with at least 50 to 70 percent fine fescue, including one or more varieties of red, chewings, hard, and sheep fescue. Never use more than 50 percent of the low-maintenance Kentucky bluegrasses or 15 percent perennial ryegrass.

Mow this type of low-maintenance lawn in late spring when the seedheads appear. Cut the grass back to 4 inches. Mow every two to four weeks, depending on your preference, cutting the grass back to 4 inches. Fertilize once or twice a year, remove noxious and woody weeds, and manage leaves as described above.

Low-Maintenance Grass Seed Cultivars

FESCUES				KENTUCKY BLUEGRASS
Chewings	Hard	Red	Sheep	
Ambassador	4001	Dawson	Azay	American
Banner III	Attilla	Jasper II	Quatro	Blue Chip
Intrigue	Bighorn	Seabreeze		Caliber
Sandpiper	Defiant			Chicago II
Shadow II	Discovery			Julia
Tiffany	Heron			Liberator
Treazure	Minotaur			Livingston
	Nordic			Merit
	Osprey			Nassau
	Oxford			NuBlue
	Reliant II			Rambo
	Rescue 911			Rugby II
	Scaldis			Unique
				Washington

(adapted from the University of Wisconsin Extension Publication A3435 *Lawn Maintenance and Problems* by Dr. John Stier)

Selecting a Quality Grass Seed

Once you decide on the desired percentages of bluegrass, fescue, and ryegrass in the mix, you need to consider the cultivars of each. Look for cultivars that provide the color and texture you desire. Then look for those best suited to the growing conditions and your level of maintenance. Use the most pest-resistant cultivars available.

Select a grass seed with several of the desired, most pest resistant, varieties of each species. This is considered a blended mix. The best contain three to five varieties of each species (bluegrass, fescue, ryegrass) used in the mix. Look for endophyte enhanced varieties of ryegrass and fescue. These contain a fungus that helps deter surface-feeding insects such as chinch bugs and sod webworms. Unfortunately they have no effect on grubs and other subsurface feeders.

We include many suitable cultivars here, but new cultivars are always being introduced. Check the Internet and your local University Extension Service for the latest information on turfgrass varieties best suited to your area. Make a list of the most pest-resistant cultivars that meet your needs, then check garden centers, feed mills, or other companies specializing in turf products. Availability may be the limiting factor that determines your selection.

All this sounds fine until you visit the garden center and try to decide which lawn seed mix is best for your situation. The front of the bag provides the first clue—Sun Mix, Shade Mix, or Play Mix. But flip to the back of the bag to differentiate a high-quality seed mix from a low-quality mix.

High-quality seed mixes have at least 90 percent purity, at least 75 percent germination for bluegrass, and at least 85 percent for fine fescues and perennial ryegrass. Purchase only certified seed, and plant it within twelve months of its test date. Certification shows that the seeds were tested and that the packaging information is correct. Noncertified seed may contain a high percentage of weed seeds, something no garden needs. Use the seed within a year to achieve the germination percentage shown on the package. As the seed ages, this germination percentage decreases, meaning fewer seeds will sprout, and the resulting lawn will be thin and sparse. You need more of the older seed to establish the lawn. Moreover, since there is no guarantee as to how quickly the germination rate decreases, you will be guessing at seeding rates and hoping for the best.

If the grass passes this test, you can start looking for other information. Select a quality seed mix with the appropriate percentages of bluegrass, fescue, and ryegrass for the light conditions in your lawn. The mix should contain several cultivars of each type of cool-season grass in the mix. Avoid grass mixes that contain annual ryegrass, *Lolium multiflorum*, also called Italian ryegrass. This grass fills in quickly, slowing establishment of the desirable grasses. After the first winter, the annual rye disappears, leaving big openings for weeds.

Don't buy grass seed that says "Variety Not Stated" or "VNS." This means you don't know what you are getting or if you are getting your money's worth. Grass seed is the cheapest part of this project. The time, water, and effort spent getting your lawn growing costs much more. So spend the extra money to get a good-quality grass seed containing named cultivars.

Look on the label at the ingredients other than grass. Inert material includes soil, chaff, and stems. The amount of such inert material should be small—don't pay for something you don't need. Other crop seeds include other grasses, such as rough bluegrass or bentgrass, that are different from those you've chosen to grow. Weed seeds are those plants we try to keep out of the lawn. So why spend money bringing in any more weeds than necessary? Quality seed mixes contain no more than 0.5 percent weed seed and 0.5 percent seeds from other crops. Never buy a grass seed containing noxious weeds.

Seeding Rates

Most lawn seed is composed of several types of grass. The seeding rates found in the individual grass profiles should be used when using a lawn seed that just contains that particular grass. Follow the seeding rates on the packages of seed mixes. If these are not available then use:

Seeding rate for new lawns:

Sun grass mix: 3 to 4 pounds of seed per 1000 square feet

Shade grass mix: 4 to 5 pounds per 1000 square feet

Overseeding rate:

Sun grass mix: 3 pounds per 1000 square feet

Shade grass mix: 4 pounds per 1000 square feet

Chapter Six

Kentucky Bluegrass

Poa pratensis

If you grew up in the Midwest or northern regions of the United States or Canada, you most likely grew up with a bluegrass lawn. The pleasing look, adaptability, and suitability of this grass species to the cooler northern climate make it the popular choice for northern lawns.

The medium to dark green of this grass species has set the standard for most lawn lovers. The desirable color, fine texture (narrow leaf blade), and tolerance to mowing make it a good choice for the manicured lawn. Moreover, its ability to spread by rhizomes (underground stems) allows the plants to fill in thin and bare spots, providing a denser stand of grass more quickly than bunch-type grasses.

Good looks are not all bluegrass has going for it. It thrives during the cool temperatures found here in spring, early summer, fall, and early winter. Lawns go dormant and turn brown during the extreme heat and drought of summer and cold of winter. But your northern lawn stays green most of the time the snow is off the ground. And the sight of spring bulbs and greening grass can make the memory of even the longest winter start to fade.

Bluegrass prefers full sun though it will tolerate a little dappled shade. Shade-tolerant bluegrass cultivars are just more shade tolerant than other bluegrass cultivars, not other shade-tolerant grass species, such as the fescues. Get the best results growing bluegrass in well-drained soil.

Kentucky Bluegrass

Facts

Growing Height—$2^1/_2$ to $3^1/_2$ inches

Mow When Grass Reaches—
3 to $4^1/_2$ inches

Soil pH—6.0 to 7.0

Drought Tolerance—poor, goes dormant

Salt Tolerance—poor

Shade Tolerance—poor, tolerates light dappled shade

Heat Tolerance—poor, goes dormant

Cold Tolerance—excellent

Cold Hardiness—3

Wear Tolerance—moderate

Spreading Rate—medium, spreads by rhizomes

Color—deep green

Texture—fine

Planting Methods and Rates

Seeding Rate—1 to $1^1/_2$ pounds per 1,000 square feet for new lawns

Overseeding Rate—1 pound per 1,000 square feet for thinning lawns

Germination Time—14 to 21 days

Sod—Divide the square footage of the area to be sodded by 9 to calculate the number of sod rolls needed.

Optimum Planting Time—Late Aug.-Sept. (mid-Oct. in south) is best or early spring before soil reaches 50 degrees Fahrenheit

Advantages

Nice color

Fine texture

Suited to cool northern climate

Cold hardy

Recovers after extreme heat, drought, and cold periods

Disadvantages

Not heat and drought tolerant

Disease problems can occur in bad weather or when lawn is mismanaged

Not salt tolerant

Slow to establish from seed

Primary Pests

Insects: Japanese beetle

Other white grubs

Sod webworm

Chinchbug

Green aphid

Diseases: Helminthosporium leaf spot

Necrotic ring spot

Snowmold

Rust

Summer patch

Other: Skunks and raccoons digging for grubs

Vole runways during winter

Mole tunnels in summer

See the appendix for a list of cultivars.

Creeping Red Fescue

Festuca rubra

This is one of several fine fescues used in shade and low-maintenance grass seed mixes. It has long been mixed with bluegrass to create more shade- and drought-tolerant seed mixes. The creeping red fescue dominates shade areas while bluegrass populates sun areas. Creeping red fescue's texture and color are similar to bluegrass, helping create a uniform appearance throughout the sun and shade areas of the lawn.

This fescue is often used in low-maintenance or no-mow mixes. It can be allowed to grow throughout the season with minimal or no mowing. No-mow lawns produce flowers that some gardeners enjoy though others find them unsightly. If allowed to grow, the grass will bend over, providing a meadow-like appearance. If you mow, cut it just as the grass starts to bloom. Mow once a month to 4 inches to maintain a more lawn-like appearance.

Most often, creeping red fescue is just one of several grasses used in traditional grass seed mixes. Other fine fescues that are more heat tolerant and disease resistant than the creeping red have been added to traditional and low-maintenance grass seed mixes. Creeping red fescue, like other grasses in lawn mixes, can be mowed and managed in a more traditional manner.

Creeping Red Fescue

Facts

Growing Height—2 to 4 inches

Mow When Grass Reaches—
3 to 6 inches

Soil pH—5.5 to 7.0

Drought Tolerance—good

Salt Tolerance—poor

Shade Tolerance—excellent
(dry shade)

Heat Tolerance—fair

Cold Tolerance—excellent

Cold Hardiness—3

Wear Tolerance—fair

Spreading Rate—slow to medium

Color—deep green

Texture—extremely fine

Advantages

Shade tolerant

Drought tolerant

Suitable for no-mow and
low-maintenance lawns

Good color

Fine texture

Blends well with bluegrass

Creeping growth habit helps in
establishment and in filling
bare areas

Endophyte types available for pest
resistance

Suited for northern climate

Disadvantages

Not as heat tolerant as other fine fescues

Does not fill in as quickly as bluegrass

Planting Methods and Rates

Seeding Rate—$3^1/2$ to $4^1/2$ pounds
per 1,000 square feet

Overseeding Rate—3 pounds per
1,000 square feet

Germination Time—7 to 10 days

Sod—Most sod is bluegrass.
Occasionally, you can find "shade"
sod with some fescue in the mix.

Optimum Planting Time—Late
Aug.-mid-Sept. (Oct. in south) is
best or early spring before soil
temperatures reach 50 degrees

Primary Pests

Insects:	(generally few problems)
	Japanese beetle
	Other white grubs
	Sod webworm
	Green aphid
Diseases:	(generally few)
	Helminthosporium leaf spot
	Necrotic ring spot
	Rust
Other:	Skunks and raccoons digging for grubs
	Vole runways during winter
	Mole tunnels in summer

See the appendix for a list of cultivars.

Hard Fescue

Festuca longifolia

Hard fescue is another type of fine fescue that can be found in both shade and low-maintenance lawn seed mixes. Like the other fine fescues, it is shade and drought tolerant, and overall more heat, drought, and disease tolerant. As a result, it is increasingly commonplace in seed mixes.

All the fine fescues tend to dominate the shade areas of the lawn while the bluegrass takes over in the sunnier areas. They also bring more drought tolerance, keeping the lawn green longer during periods of drought.

Unlike creeping red, hard fescue tends to grow in bunches, making it slower to fill in and blend with bluegrass than creeping red and chewings fescues. The bunch-type growth habit also makes it slower to repopulate bare areas after extensive wear.

Look for low-maintenance and shady grass mixes that contain several species of fine fescue. Adding hard fescue to the mix can increase your lawn's tolerance to heat and disease. This is the best species for low-maintenance lawns.

Hard Fescue

Facts

Growing Height—2 to 4 inches

Mow When Grass Reaches—
3 to 6 inches

Soil pH—5.5 to 7.0

Drought Tolerance—good

Salt Tolerance—poor

Shade Tolerance—excellent (dry)

Heat Tolerance—fair, better than other fine fescues

Cold Tolerance—excellent

Cold Hardiness—3

Wear Tolerance—fair

Spreading Rate—slow, bunch-type

Color—deep green

Texture—extremely fine

Planting Methods and Rates

Seeding Rate—3$^1/_2$ to 4$^1/_2$ pounds per 1,000 square feet

Overseeding Rate—3 pounds per 1,000 square feet

Germination Time—7 to 10 days

Sod—Most sod is bluegrass. Occasionally you can find "shade" sod with some fescue in the mix.

Optimum Planting Time— Late Aug.-Sept. (mid-Oct. in south) is best or early spring before soil temperatures reach 50 degrees

Advantages

Shade tolerant

Drought tolerant

Cold tolerant

Hardy

More disease resistant than creeping red

More heat tolerant than creeping red

Disadvantages

Bunch-type grower

Slow to establish and spread

Slow to recover from wear

Primary Pests

Insects: (generally few if any)
Japanese beetle
Other white grubs
Sod webworm
Green aphid

Diseases: Helminthosporium leaf spot
Rust

Other: Skunks and raccoons digging for grubs
Vole runways during winter
Mole tunnels in summer

See the appendix for a list of cultivars.

Chapter Six

Chewings Fescue

Festuca rubra var. *commutata*

The common fine fescues now used in shade and low-maintenance lawn mixes contain chewings, as well as creeping red and hard fescue. Chewings is much like creeping red fescue, but it tends to grow more as a bunch grass than a spreader. This makes it even slower to fill in bare areas and recover from wear.

Chewings fescue has long been used as a pasture grass. It can also be found along roadsides and in athletic turfgrass mixes. Its drought and shade tolerance make it suitable for use in home lawns. Chewings can be allowed to grow long when used in a no-mow lawn mix or mowed shorter for a more traditional lawn.

Select a lawn seed mix that includes this and other fine fescues. Using a mixture of fescue species and varieties provides greater diversity in the lawn. That means the grass will withstand extremes in weather and growing conditions while having better pest resistance.

Chewings Fescue

Facts

Growing Height—2 to 4 inches

Mow When Grass Reaches—
3 to 6 inches

Soil pH—5.5 to 7.0

Drought Tolerance—good

Salt Tolerance—poor

Shade Tolerance—excellent
(dry shade)

Heat Tolerance—fair

Cold Tolerance—excellent

Cold Hardiness—3

Wear Tolerance—fair

Spreading Rate—slow, bunch-type

Color—deep green

Texture—extremely fine

Advantages

Shade tolerant

Drought tolerant

Suitable for no-mow and
low-maintenance lawns

Will tolerate close mowing

Good color

Fine texture

Blends well with bluegrass

Endophyte types available for pest
resistance

Suited for Northern climate

Disadvantages

Slow to fill in and become established

Slow to recover from wear

Planting Methods and Rates

Seeding Rate—3$\frac{1}{2}$ to 4$\frac{1}{2}$ pounds
per 1,000 square feet

Overseeding Rate—3 pounds per
1,000 square feet

Germination Time—7 to 10 days

Sod—Most sod is bluegrass.
Occasionally, you can find "shade"
sod with some fescue in the mix.
Divide the square footage of the
area to be sodded by 9 to calculate
the number of sod rolls needed.

Optimum Planting Time—Late
Aug.-Sept. (mid-Oct. in south) is
best or early spring before soil
temperatures reach 50 degrees

Primary Pests

Insects:	(generally few problems)
	Japanese beetle
	Other white grubs
	Sod webworm
	Green aphid
Diseases:	(generally few)
	Helminthosporium leaf spot
	Necrotic ring spot
	Rust
Other:	Skunks and raccoons digging for grubs
	Vole runways during winter
	Mole tunnels in summer

See the appendix for a list of cultivars.

Tall Fescue

Festuca arundinacea

This grass is the answer for homeowners looking for a drought-tolerant, low-maintenance grass that produces a medium-quality lawn. The lighter green and coarser texture give it a less refined look than the typical bluegrass lawn. But its drought tolerance and low fertilizer requirements make it a good choice for lawns growing in sandy soils, at a weekend cabin, and in other areas where water and time for lawn care may be limited.

First introduced to this country from Europe in the early 1800s, tall fescue was mainly used as a pasture grass throughout the United States. The deep and extensive root system makes it drought tolerant and able to stay green through most of the growing season. It will go dormant under extreme heat and drought but will recover with cooler temperatures and irrigation.

Recent breeding efforts have focused on developing turf-type tall fescues. These cultivars have narrower leaves, form denser stands, and have better green throughout the summer.

Use turf-type tall fescues to create a low-maintenance, drought-tolerant lawn. Do not mix these with other grasses since their growth habit, texture, and color do not mix well with other lawn grasses.

Tall Fescue

Facts

Growing Height—2^1/$_2$ to 3^1/$_2$ inches

Mow When Grass Reaches—
3 to 4^1/$_2$ inches

Soil pH—5.0 to 8.5

Drought Tolerance—good

Salt Tolerance—fair

Shade Tolerance—good

Heat Tolerance—good

Cold Tolerance—good

Cold Hardiness—4, some hardiness problems in northern regions

Wear Tolerance—good

Spreading Rate—medium, bunch type

Color—medium green

Texture—medium to coarse

Planting Methods and Rates

Seeding Rate—7 to 9 pounds per 1,000 square feet for new lawns

Overseeding Rate—6 pounds per 1,000 square feet for thinning lawns

Germination Time—7 to 10 days

Sod—Limited availability throughout the Midwest. Standard sod is 1^1/$_2$ feet wide by 6 feet long covering 9 square feet of lawn. Divide the square footage of the area to be sodded by 9 to calculate the number of sod rolls needed.

Optimum Planting Time—Mid-May-June

Advantages

Drought tolerant

Low maintenance

Forms a medium-quality lawn with minimal care

Suited to cool northern climate

Cold hardy

Fair salt tolerance

Endophyte type seeds provide pest resistance

Disadvantages

Coarse texture

Does not mix well with other lawn grasses

Slow to fill in bare and thinned areas

Primary Pests

Insects: White grubs

Diseases: Helminthosporium leaf spot
Necrotic ring spot
Rust

Other: Skunks and raccoons digging for grubs
Vole runways during winter
Mole tunnels in summer

See the appendix for a list of cultivars.

Perennial Ryegrass

Lolium perenne

R yegrass has long been included in both sunny and shady lawn seed mixes. These fast-germinating grasses provide quick cover, prevent erosion, and serve as a living mulch until the slower germinating fescues and bluegrass sprout.

Annual ryegrass was the choice grass of the past. It's cheap and serves as a temporary filler. Unfortunately, it often dominates the lawn the first season, limiting the growth of fescue and bluegrass plants. Once it dies over winter, annual ryegrass leaves the new lawn full of bare spots. Weeds often move in before the bluegrass and fescues have a chance. Do not purchase lawn seed mixes containing annual ryegrass (which is often called Italian ryegrass).

But the newer turf-type perennial ryegrass is better suited for lawn establishment. It has the same attributes as the annual ryegrass but stays in the lawn, allowing for a smoother, less weedy transition into a bluegrass-fescue lawn. The finer leaf blade and darker color help this grass blend better with the bluegrass and fescues.

The high level of pest resistance and wearability of perennial ryegrass are added benefits. These features have made it a leading choice for athletic fields. It can also be used to overseed high-traffic areas for quick repair and durability.

Turf-type perennial ryegrass is becoming a larger part of home lawn seed mixes. Some lawn owners use 100 percent ryegrass in high-traffic areas. They reseed yearly or as needed to fill in the thin areas. Perennial rye may be damaged in extreme winters in northern parts of the Midwest. Use mixes with smaller percentages of rye in these areas.

Perennial Ryegrass

Facts

Growing Height—2 to 3$\frac{1}{2}$ inches

Mow When Grass Reaches—
3 to 4$\frac{1}{2}$ inches

Soil pH—6.0 to 7.0

Drought Tolerance—poor

Salt Tolerance—fair

Shade Tolerance—fair

Heat Tolerance—fair

Cold Tolerance—poor

Cold Hardiness—3, may suffer winter injury in far north

Wear Tolerance—good

Spreading Rate—slow, bunch-type

Color—deep green

Texture—medium

Planting Methods and Rates

Seeding Rate—7 to 9 pounds per 1,000 square feet for new lawns

Overseeding Rate—7 pounds per 1,000 square feet for thinning lawns

Germination Time—5 to 7 days

Sod—not available

Optimum Planting Time—Mid- to late August through mid-September in northern states and mid-October in southern regions of the Midwest are the best. Or early spring before soil temperatures reach 50 degrees.

Advantages

Quick cover

Aids in establishment of lawns

Wearability

Turf-types blend with other cool-season grasses

Some salt tolerance

Pest resistant

Endophyte types available for added pest resistance

Disadvantages

May suffer winter injury in extreme winters of nothern Midwest

Primary Pests

Insects: (generally few)
Japanese beetle
Other white grubs
Sod webworm
Chinchbug

Diseases: Helminthosporium leaf spot
Rust

Other: Skunks and raccoons digging for grubs
Vole runways during winter
Mole tunnels in summer

See the appendix for a list of cultivars.

85

Other Grass Varieties to Know

Other Bluegrasses

Rough, *Poa trivialis*, and supina, *Poa supina*, bluegrasses are often considered weeds when they invade bluegrass and fescue lawns. Their light green color makes them easy to spot in a dark green bluegrass and fescue lawn. They may, however, be the perfect grass for moist and poorly drained conditions where standard grasses won't grow. You'll have to do some looking to find these moisture-tolerant bluegrasses. Try searching the Internet or contacting a turf supply company in your area. Though hard to find, they are well worth the effort and extra money if you want to grow grass in these less-than-ideal soil conditions. Supina also tolerates and grows in high-traffic areas.

Sow seeds of rough bluegrass at a rate of 1 to $1^1/_2$ pounds per 1,000 square feet and supina bluegrass at a rate of $1^1/_4$ to $1^1/_2$ pounds per 1,000 square feet. Use a mixture of at least 20 percent rough bluegrass and at least 10 percent supina bluegrass. These grasses are more moisture tolerant than the major cool-season grasses. Add no more than 40 percent fescue and no more than 40 percent bluegrass to the mix. Use more bluegrass than fescue for moist sunny areas and more fescue than bluegrass for moist shady areas. Finish off the mix with less than 15 percent ryegrass.

Buffalograss

Buffalograss, *Buchloe dactyloides*, is native to the short-grass prairies of the North American Great Plains. This slow-growing, drought-tolerant grass requires little fertilization. It has been used in warmer regions along roadsides, and new varieties are being introduced for use in non-play areas of some southern golf courses. Limited applications have been tried throughout the Midwest with varying results. It is slow to establish and not reliably hardy in the north. So don't get too excited; limit use to small experimental areas. Left unmowed and allowed to flower, buffalograss reaches heights of 6 to 8 inches. If you mow, cut it when it reaches 3 to 4 inches to maintain a 2- to 3-inch turf. This slow-growing grass requires less frequent mowing and less water than bluegrass lawns. Buffalograss "seed" is really a burr that contains several seeds. Deburred seed is much harder to find and more expensive. Sow the burrs at a rate of 1 to 3 pounds per 1,000 square feet and $1/_2$ inch deep.

There are many turfgrass options available. When choosing a grass for your lawn, consider your regional conditions, your particular site, availability at local stores, personal preferences in grass texture and appearance, anticipated use of the lawn, maintenance requirements, and pest resistance.

Zoysiagrass

According to the ads that pop up everywhere in spring, zoysiagrass, *Zoysia* spp., is too good to be true. And it is. The ads say this heat- and drought-tolerant grass stays green during the hottest months of summer, requires minimal mowing, and out-competes the weeds. What the ads don't mention is your lawn will be brown for the other ten months of the year. This southern grass should *not* be planted in the Midwest. It is not reliably hardy, though I have seen several zoysia lawns in Wisconsin. If it does survive, it is almost impossible to kill. You will have to repeatedly apply a total vegetation killer in late summer followed by sodding or seeding. So avoid the temptation: stick with cool-season grasses more suited to the Midwest.

87

Common Turfgrass Pests

Chapter Seven

- **Be Observant for Changes in Your Lawn**
- **Watch for Symptoms and Signs**
- **Gauge the Proper Time for Action**
- **Use a Process of Elimination to Identify the Problem**
- **Follow Good Management Practices as the First Line of Defense**
- **Spot Treat if Possible**
- **Use Chemicals as a Last Resort**

A beautiful lawn means different things to different gardeners. Some picture a sea of fine deep green grass free of weeds, insects, and disease. Others, like me, are willing to tolerate some imperfections as long as the grass is generally healthy and green. No matter what your vision of a perfect lawn, we all want it with the least amount of work and problems. If you follow the advice on selection, planting, and care, you'll avoid most problems. A healthy lawn is your best defense against insects, weeds, and diseases. But sometimes, no matter what you do, the weather stresses the lawn, diseases attack, or insects move in and damage the lawn. We use a Plant Health Care approach to managing these problems.

Plant Health Care

Plant Health Care is a more holistic, horticulture-focused version of Integrated Pest Management. This approach to managing pests involves proper plant selection and care to avoid problems. When problems do occur, we look for long-term, environmentally friendly solutions. This is the approach discussed here to managing weeds, insects, and diseases in the lawn. Pest management starts before you have a problem. Review your management strategies. As described in previous chapters, keep the grass at least $2^1/_2$ to $3^1/_2$ inches tall. Mow often enough so you remove only one-third of the grass blade at each cutting. Fertilize at the right time using products recommended by your soil test report.

Monitor your lawn for problems. Discovering a problem when it is small makes it much easier to control than it will be once it has had time to reproduce and take over. Violets are a perfect example. One pretty violet looks innocent enough—until it flowers and produces seeds. When the seeds ripen, the plant shoots them all over the lawn. These new colonies of weeds grow larger in diameter and produce more seeds. Soon you are growing a garden of violets instead of a bluegrass lawn. When problems are caught early, you can dig or spot-treat the few problem plants rather than repairing the whole yard.

Use a notebook or garden journal to record significant weather such as drought, excess rain, and extreme heat and cold. Changes in the weather can damage the lawn or lead to pest problems. Sometimes control is just a matter of waiting for better weather, but other times you may need to take action to control the disease or insect population. Consider recording dates of fertilizer, herbicide, and other chemical applications. Improper applications or bad timing can cause damage to the turf. As with bad weather, you may have to wait for the grass to outgrow the damage. In severe cases, you may need to do some overseeding.

Once a problem occurs, take a closer look at the grass and the growing conditions. Check for thatch buildup, waterlogged soil, spots on the leaves, and other signs of insects and diseases. Review weather patterns and maintenance practices to help you diagnose the problem. Evaluate the pattern of damage and the timeframe in which it occurred. Are there large irregular patches of dead grass or small circular spots of brown grass? Did the symptoms develop and spread slowly over the season or seem to appear overnight? These are all clues that will help your diagnosis.

Now look at the individual grass plants. Tug on the brown grass to see whether the roots are intact. Grubs and root rots can damage roots, making it easy to remove the dead blades. Look at the green grass blades growing next to the brown or dead patches. These often show spots, discoloration, and other symptoms of the problem. When someone brings me a patch of dead grass, about all I can tell is that it's dead. But if the section contains both living and dead grass, I can usually find the symptoms and start looking for the cause. You can do the same.

Once you have identified the symptoms, you can start looking for the culprit that caused the damage. Check out the profiles of lawn pests included in this chapter. These are the most common problems found on Midwest lawns. If your lawn's problem does not match these, consult your local University Extension Service, garden center, or lawn care professional. All your record keeping and digging for clues will help the experts diagnose the problem quickly and more accurately.

Diagnosis is just the beginning of the process. Find out all you can about the pest, the short- and long-term impacts on your lawn, and the consequences of treatment for the grass, you, and the environment. Nature or a change in maintenance can minimize many lawn problems. Others, more serious, may warrant your intervention. Select the most environmentally friendly control option available. Look for solutions that do not injure the good bugs or good microorganisms that help keep the soil and plants healthy. Minimizing the negative impact on the environment by working with nature means a healthier lawn and fewer problems for you to manage in the future.

Always record and evaluate the success of any control. You may need to adjust the timing or try something different. This useful information may help you avoid future problems or skip the experimental stage by recording the lessons learned in past seasons. Mark next year's calendar as a reminder to watch for symptoms. Catching the problem early will make your job easier.

Pest Problem Questionnaire

If the problem isn't obvious, you may need to search a little more. The following questions may help uncover the clues to your lawn's problem. Matching the answers with the pests described in this chapter will help lead you to a proper diagnosis and treatment.

- *What are the symptoms, both above ground on the leaves and below ground on the roots?*

- *Use a knife to dig in and look at the thatch layer and roots. Check out the grass blades located in and surrounding the damaged areas.*

- *Are there spots, lesions, or discolorations on the individual leaf blades?*

- *Is the root system healthy with lots of white fibrous roots? If not, are the roots stunted, slimy, chewed, or missing? Do they have holes or a distinct color?*

- *Is there a thatch layer? If so, how thick?*

- *Does the problem have a distinct pattern? Is it a smattering of small circles or one large patch? Are the affected areas irregularly shaped or indistinct? Or does the lawn appear streaked?*

- *Is the problem concentrated in one area of the lawn or scattered throughout? Do the growing conditions, light, and moisture vary from the damaged areas to the healthy portions of the lawn?*

- *When did the problem appear? Did the damage seem to coincide with any change in weather or care?*

- *What type of grass are you growing? Is it receiving the light, moisture, and care it prefers?*

Now review your maintenance program:

- *When did you have you soil tested? Are you fertilizing based on soil test results or the "best guess" method?*

- *When did you last fertilize and with what?*

- *Have you used any weed killers on the lawn? If so, how much of what product was used?*

- *Are you mowing frequently and high, at least $2^1/_2$ to $3^1/_2$ inches?*

- *Have you sharpened your mower blade?*

- *When and how often do you water the lawn?*

Look for surprises:

- *Have you checked underground for buried boards, old patios, or other items that may interfere with drainage and moisture retention?*

- *Did you or your neighbor recently drain the swimming pool on your lawn?*

- *Did you spill gas, oil, paint cleaner, or fertilizer in the damaged area?*

- *Did you use a chemical to kill the weeds in the driveway or patio?*

- *Is the damage near a septic tank or sewer drainage line?*

Troubleshooting Symptoms

Scenario 1—Grass affected in distinct circular patterns

Symptoms	Possible Causes
Ring of dark green grass with mushrooms	Fairy ring
Leaves chewed	Armyworms
Small bleached spots or circles	Dollar spot
Brown patch with tuft of green grass in center	Necrotic ring spot
Small brown patches	Dog urine
Brown grass with dead dandelion in center	Misuse of pesticide

Scenario 2—Grass affected in irregular patterns

Symptoms	Possible Causes
Slow decline, yellowish area, shallow roots, wilt	Nematodes
Leaves have gray cast, turn yellow-brown then slimy, and mat together	Pythium
Grass comes out of winter matted white to brown and sometimes covered with pink or gray fuzz	Snowmold
Yellowish spots with fuzzy orange lesions and shoes "turn" orange when you cross the lawn	Rust
White powdery substance on leaves	Powdery mildew
Spots on leaves, grass browns and melts away	Helminthosporium leaf spot
Yellowish or dead spots, grass easily pulls out, no roots	Billbugs
Center dead, yellowish brown grass	Chinch bugs
Grass blades cut and webbing near surface	Sod webworms
Grass fades or soil dries quickly	Septic tank, buried patio, or change in soil texture
Weak, thin, leggy grass	Excess shade
Grass thin, wilts quickly, fertilizer doesn't help	Competition with trees
Brown grass along walks and drives in spring	De-icing salt
Runways of dead grass in spring	Voles
Ridges in lawn in summer	Moles

Scenario 3—Grass affected in streaked patterns

Symptoms	Possible Causes
Grass bleached, yellow, brown, or dead	Chemical burn (fertilizer, herbicide, etc.)

Scenario 4—Grass affected but no particular pattern

Symptoms	Possible Causes
Roots cut off, dead areas in lawn, grass pulls up easily	*Grubs*
Stems chewed near soil surface, wilting and dead	*Cutworms*
Grass bleached or speckled, hopping insects	*Leafhoppers*
Small mounds or lines of disturbed soil	*Ants*
Grass blades covered with gray chalky substance	*Slime mold*
Grass spongy	*Thatch*
Weeds	*Compaction, shade, wet soils, poor management*
Grass has grayish cast, tips of leaves split or frayed	*Dull mower blade*
Grass thin, weak, and doesn't respond to proper care	*Variety not suited to location*
Grass yellowish green on older blades, eventually brown tips	*Nitrogen deficiency*
Yellowish foliage, especially new growth or between veins	*Iron deficiency, high pH*
Grass grayish green to brown, leaves rolled, soil dry	*Drought*
Yellow, thin blades and weak roots	*Excessive water*

Weeds

You've seen them, pulled them, and probably cursed a few—weeds. These unwelcome plants grow where they aren't wanted. Dandelion, crabgrass, and thistle are just a few of these uninvited guests found in many lawns. Keep your lawn thick and healthy, and you make it harder for these weeds to get a roothold in your lawn. Keep the grass tall to shade out weed seeds and prevent them from sprouting and taking over. Water and fertilize your way to a dense lawn that is able to crowd out intruders.

When weeds move in, it is time to evaluate the growing conditions and maintenance practices. Weeds are good indicator plants, letting you know when the weather, soil, light, or management practices are not right. Weeds are able to out-compete lawn grasses in less than ideal conditions. Correct the problem, and you minimize the number of weeds and the need for herbicides. But if left unchecked, weeds start seeding, spreading, and taking over. Soon you can't see the grass for the weeds. Check the lawn often for signs of unwanted plants. It is easy to dig one or two dandelions. But once these plants flower and release hundreds of seeds, you'll be weeding out twenty, thirty, or more weeds next season.

Once the weeds are established, you may need to step in with chemicals for short-term relief. Spot-treat problem areas instead of treating the whole lawn. This reduces your use of pesticides, which is good for both the environment and your wallet. If weeds make up 50 percent or more of your lawn, you may want to start over. Killing off the existing lawn, weeds and all, may be less work and require fewer chemicals than trying to reclaim your lawn from all those weeds.

Understanding weeds makes it easier to select the best method of control. Lawn weeds include annual, biennial, and perennial grass and broadleaf plants. Annuals like crabgrass grow from seed, flower, produce seed, and die in one season. Biennials need two years to complete their lifecycle. They start from seed and produce a small rosette of leaves the first season. The second season they flower, seed, and die. Perennial weeds such as dandelions produce leaves the first season. Then they flower, seed, and survive for several or many seasons.

Grassy weeds have narrow leaves with parallel veins. They look similar to the lawn grasses but have an undesirable appearance, size, or growth habit. This makes them stand out among the lawn's bluegrass and fescues.

Broadleaf weeds have wider leaves with netted veins. The vascular system, or vessels that carry water and nutrients, in these plants is arranged differently than in grass plants. This difference is what makes broadleaf weed killers able to kill broadleaf plants without harming grass.

Sedges are grass-like plants. The leaf blades are narrow and often light green and shiny. Able to tolerate wet soils, they are often found in lawns with poor drainage. Their triangular stems give rise to a plant identification rhyme: "sedges have edges."

Controlling Annual Grass Weeds

Crabgrass is the most troublesome annual grass weed in Midwest lawns. This warm-weather weed moves into lawns stressed by summer heat and drought. As the lawn grasses thin or go dormant, the crabgrass thrives, produces seeds, and starts filling in voids in the lawn. The cycle starts in early spring, April to early May, when the crabgrass seeds sprout. Seeds can sprout as late as early July. By midsummer, you'll notice the rosette of light green leaves filling the thin or bare areas of the lawn. By late summer, the grass goes to seed and then disappears by fall.

Keep your grass tall, $2^1/_2$ to $3^1/_2$ inches, to shade the ground and prevent the seeds from sprouting. Proper watering and fertilization keep your lawn dense and healthy so it can crowd out any crabgrass plants that manage to sprout. If this doesn't work, you may want to use chemicals to get the problem under control. Apply a pre-emergent crabgrass killer in April or early May, when the soil temperatures reach about 50 degrees Fahrenheit. This is about the same time the bridal wreath spirea is about to bloom. Do not use a pre-emergent herbicide if you are planning on reseeding your lawn. These products will prevent your lawn grass seed from germinating, as well. Look for a product containing the active ingredient Tupersan® if you must use a pre-emergent and reseed in spring. This product has a shorter waiting period between application and seeding.

Apply pre-emergent crabgrass killer to areas infested in the past. Increase the area by several feet to compensate for spreading seed. Adjust your management practices, and soon you will be able to eliminate the pesticide and keep crabgrass in check. The new corn gluten products are good alternatives for people who want a more environmentally friendly chemical control. The University of Iowa found corn gluten suppressed germination of crabgrass and other weed seeds. It takes several years of applications to reduce weeds by 50 percent or more. Many lawn owners have reported satisfactory results reducing weeds while addressing their concern for pets and children playing on the lawn. Post-emergent products are also available. These are expensive, and timing is critical for success. Acclaim® and Dimension® can be applied to crabgrass plants when they are young.

Crabgrass

Perennial Grass Weeds

Quack grass, bentgrass, coarse fescue, and other perennial grass weeds present a greater challenge. Like crabgrass, they move into thin and bare areas where the lawn is stressed. Unlike crabgrass, no chemical will kill them without harming your lawn. This makes control difficult, time consuming, and very frustrating.

Keep these weed grasses out by using quality grass seed whenever seeding or overseeding the lawn. Poor-quality grass seed has a higher percentage of weed seeds that can include these grasses. Proper care will also give your lawn grasses the competitive edge over these weeds.

Quack Grass   **Coarse Fescue**

Once the weeds get established, remove the weed grass and reseed the area with the desirable lawn grass. Some weeds, such as bentgrass and coarse fescue, can be readily removed by hand. Dig out the grass roots with an inch of soil and reseed. Others, such as quack grass, are efficient at spreading and require more attention. That long white "root" you see when pulling quack grass is really a rhizome. Any piece of this that breaks off and touches soil can start a new plant.

Spot-treat areas infested by quack grass with a total vegetation killer such as Roundup® or Finale®. Some of these products are absorbed by the leaves and move into the roots, killing the whole plant. Use these products carefully since they can kill anything green that they touch, including your lawn. Read and follow all label directions. Remove the dead grass, prepare the soil, and reseed within one to two weeks. These products can be used to spot-treat and kill any of the weed grasses. Some gardeners prefer to use products containing the active ingredient cacodylic acid, olive oil, or vinegar. These naturally derived products burn only the tops of the plants. They are considered more environmentally friendly but do not kill the roots. Several applications are needed to kill perennial weeds with an established root system. Be careful—these products too can damage any green plant they touch, including your lawn.

Annual Broadleaf Weeds

Pull or dig annual broadleaf weeds, such as henbit and annual chickweed, as soon as they appear. Removing them before they mature and set seed reduces future populations and future work for you.

Summer annuals sprout in spring with the crabgrass seed. Many of their seeds will be controlled by your pre-emergent crabgrass application. Winter annuals, whose seeds sprout in late summer or fall, are usually managed by your perennial broadleaf weed control.

Henbit

Chickweed

Perennial Broadleaf Weeds

Dandelions, plantain, clover, and violets are just a few of the broadleaf weeds that like to make their home in your lawn. Evaluate and improve the growing conditions so your lawn is able to crowd out the weeds. Dig and remove the few weeds that may accidentally seed into your lawn. At a minimum, remove flowers and seedheads to prevent the weeds from spreading.

Pre-emergent herbicides, including corn gluten, kill some of the broadleaf weed seeds. They won't eliminate the existing plants but may reduce the number of new ones sprouting. You may decide to use chemicals on larger populations or spreading infestations that can't be managed by digging. Spot-treat problem weeds with a broadleaf weedkiller. Read and follow all label directions. These products can damage nearby flowers, trees, and shrubs if misapplied. Larger infestations scattered throughout the lawn may require a total lawn application. As the populations decrease and the health of your lawn improves, you can reduce both the treatment area and the number of applications. One application every three to five years is sufficient to keep weed populations low.

Dandelion   **Thistle**

Plantain

Early to mid-May or early to mid-September are the best times to control most perennial broadleaf weeds. Timing may vary and can make the difference between control and wasted effort. Check out the specifics for the difficult weeds discussed below.

Moss and Mushrooms

They're not your typical weed plants, but moss and mushrooms often appear in lawns. Both are difficult to eliminate, and doing so requires patience and special management.

Mushrooms seem to appear mysteriously in the lawn after a rainy spell. They are the fruiting bodies of fungi that live in the soil. The fungus feeds on decaying wood from tree roots, stumps, boards, or similar materials in the ground. Once the weather dries, the mushrooms die, but the fungus continues its work below ground level. Time and patience are your best control mechanisms. Once the food source—decaying wood—has decomposed, the fungus and mushrooms have no food and will disappear. In the meantime, rake the sprouting mushrooms to prevent children and pets from eating them. Prostar fungicide drench may provide control. See Fairy Ring in the Disease section for more mushroom-related information.

Mushroom

Moss is a problem in shade and in compacted, poorly drained soils. Correct the growing conditions, and you eliminate this unwanted plant. Most chemicals labeled for controlling moss just burn off the plant. The moss will return if the growing conditions are not corrected

Improve soil drainage by core aeration and addition of organic matter. Lime is often recommended as a cure for moss, but use lime only to raise the pH of acid soils, not to cure moss problems. Follow soil test results, and never add lime to alkaline soils. Liming alkaline soils will just generate a different set of problems and more work for you. Increase the sunlight reaching the ground by hiring a certified arborist to thin dense tree canopies. Or replace the grass with more shade-tolerant ground covers or mulch. If all else fails, add a few flagstone steppers and call it a moss garden. Sometimes it is wiser and a lot less work to go along with nature than to fight a losing battle.

Difficult-to-Control Weeds

Clover once was included in grass seed mixes. Its ability to capture nitrogen from the atmosphere made it useful in the establishment of lawns. At some point, though, we decided it was a weed, no longer a valued part of the lawn, and should be eliminated. A large infestation of clover may mean you need to adjust your fertilization program. Consider taking a soil test and adjusting your lawn-care practices before reaching for the herbicide. If the problem continues, you may decide to use a chemical. Product selection and application are critical for successfully killing this plant. Select a weedkiller labeled for use on clover and other difficult weeds. Include a sticker spreader or a little detergent in the herbicide mix. This helps the product coat and stick to the waxy clover leaves for better control.

White Clover

Bindweed

A creeping vine covered with white morning glory blooms sounds beautiful—until it invades your lawn. Field bindweed is a deep-rooted perennial relative of the morning glory flower. It is difficult to kill with standard lawn weedkillers. Try some of the weedkillers labeled for bindweed and other difficult weeds. Or paint Roundup® on the leaves of this weed, being careful not to touch the grass. Several applications may be needed.

Ground ivy, also known as creeping Charlie, was brought here from Europe as a ground cover. It usually gets its start in the shade but quickly moves into other areas of the lawn. Its fragrant leaves tolerate traffic, and the purple flowers produce seed that can last for many years in the soil. Timing is the key to successfully controlling this weed. Any broadleaf weedkiller will work if applied when the plant is in full bloom or after a hard freeze in the fall. Don't be discouraged if you see this plant the following season. It will take several years to kill all the offspring lying dormant in the soil.

Ground Ivy

Violet

Avoid using weedkillers containing dicamba or Banvel® under trees and shrubs. Though the products are effective, repeat applications can injure the plants. Adjust your timing, and use other broadleaf weedkillers that are less harmful to your trees and shrubs. Some of you may have heard of using borax to control ground ivy. The University of Iowa found that ground ivy is more sensitive to boron than bluegrass is, so the idea is to kill the ground ivy by giving it an overdose of boron. Unfortunately, because thoroughly mixing the solution is difficult, many gardeners have killed both the ground ivy and their bluegrass. I also worry about the long-term impact on other nearby plants.

Violets may start in the garden, but they soon leap into the lawn, spreading by seed and root. As the seeds ripen, they shoot across the lawn, starting new colonies. Violets are pretty in bloom but frustrating if you are trying to eliminate them from your lawn. Treat unwanted violets growing in the lawn in mid-September and again in late October with a weedkiller labeled for use on violets and other difficult weeds such as Triclopyr.

Insects

Take a close look at your landscape; you may be surprised who you find living in your lawn. The healthiest, best-looking lawns are filled with insects. An estimated one hundred thousand different species of insects live in North America alone. Probably one thousand of these call your backyard their home. Fortunately, most of them are good guys—the insects that pollinate our flowers, create organic matter that improves our soil, and eat harmful insects that bother our plants, home, and health.

Those insects that are troublesome are usually kept under control by nature and proper care. The cold Midwest winters kill many of them. Combine this with our short season and summer showers, and the number drops even more. A healthy lawn can usually tolerate small infestations of insects. It quickly recovers from the damage done by insects feeding on it and does not suffer long-term damage. Adjust management practices to improve your lawn's health, along with its resistance and resilience to insect damage.

Don't apply insecticides as a preventative. This is a waste of time, money, and pesticides. Applying chemicals too far in advance may not provide control if and when the problem occurs. Preventative sprays can increase pest problems by killing the good guys that eat the lawn-damaging pests. So before you reach for a pesticide, make sure the insect you find is really causing problems. Here are some easy tests you can conduct to make sure insects are the cause of your lawn problem:

Flotation Test: This test is used for chinch bugs and other leaf-feeding insects. Remove both ends of a coffee can or similar container. Sink the can in the grass at the edge of the dead area. Fill the can with water and agitate the grass. Chinch bugs and other insects will float to the surface. Test several areas. Treatment is needed if you find two or three chinch bugs per test. Treat for other pests when their populations are causing turf damage.

Irritation Test: This test will detect sod webworm, armyworm, and cutworm larvae. Mix 1 tablespoon of dishwashing detergent in 1 gallon of water. Sprinkle the soapy water over 1 square yard of lawn. Conduct the test in several areas, both damaged spots and areas adjacent to the damaged grass. Check the treated areas several times over the next ten minutes. Treat if one or more sod webworm larvae, armyworms, or cutworms are present.

Turf Removal Test: This is done to confirm the presence of grubs. Cut out and remove 1 square foot of turf. Check the top 4 to 6 inches of soil for white grub larvae. Replace the sample and keep the soil moist until it re-roots. Treat if three to four grubs are found per 1 square foot of turf.

Use the following pest profiles to identify any insects found. Then decide what, if any, control is needed for the pest. Small populations, those completing their cycle of damage, or pests that do not negatively impact the long-term health of the plant may be left for nature to manage. You may choose to manage large numbers of turf-damaging pests. Be sure to read and follow all label directions before purchasing and using insecticides.

More and more organic insecticides are becoming available for us to use. But keep in mind that even something labeled "organic" must be used with caution. The bacteria *Bacillus thuringiensis* kills true caterpillars. This includes the larvae of the harmful sod webworm, but also those of swallowtails, monarchs, and other butterflies you may be trying to attract to the garden. Check the label to be sure the product will provide the desired results.

Neem, pyrethrins, rotenone, canola oil, and other plant-derived products are also available. Some provide very specific control, while others kill a wide spectrum of good and bad insects. Make sure the product and formula you select is labeled for use on lawns. And always wear gloves, goggles, shoes, pants, and long sleeves when applying any chemical.

Beneficial Insects

Beneficial Insect	Feeds On
Ant Lion (Doodlebug)	Caterpillars, aphids, and many other soil insects
Assassin Bug (Wheel Bug)	Assortment of insects, but can bite you also
Big-eyed Bug	Chinch bugs, assorted insect eggs, small larvae, and soft-bodied insects
Damsel Bug	Aphids, assorted insect eggs, small larvae, and many other soft-bodied insects
Earthworm*	Doesn't feed on insects but good for the soil, although too many can make the soil level lumpy. Lightly rolling moist soil can reduce uneven surface.
Earwig	Can also feed on plants, but is typically a predator and eats chinch bugs, webworms, and other soil insects
Green Lacewing (Aphid Lion)	Small caterpillars, aphids, mites, thrips, mealybugs, soft bodied insects, and insect eggs
Ground Beetle	Feeds on almost any soil insect, particularly cutworms, armyworms, sod webworms, and small mole crickets
Ladybug Beetle (Ladybird Beetle)	Adults and larvae feed on small, soft-bodied insects such as aphids, mites, scale, and insect eggs

Beneficial Insects (cont.)

Beneficial Insect	Feeds On
Minute Pirate Bug	Thrips, spider mites, and assorted insect eggs
Nematode	Beneficial nematodes (*Steinernema* and *Heterohabditis* species) can feed on assorted caterpillar larvae or grubs, and flea larvae
Parasitic Wasp	Crickets, caterpillars, and aphids
Predaceous Stinkbug	Feeds on many assorted insects including caterpillar larvae
Praying Mantis	Feeds on almost any other insect. including other beneficials
Rove Beetle	Aphids, nematodes, most soil inhabiting larvae
Spined Soldier Bug	Fall armyworm and other caterpillar larvae
Spider*	Feeds on an assortment of pests, including beetles, caterpillars, leafhoppers, and aphids
Syrphid Fly (Hover Fly)	Larval stage feeds on soft-bodied insects such as aphids

*not technically insects, but beneficial nonetheless

Learn to recognize good bugs in all their stages—a ladybug beetle larva doesn't look at all like a ladybug.

Most Wanted List (but not in your lawn)

Very few of the insects wandering through and living in your lawn create problems. Mites, aphids, and grasshoppers are common but seldom cause enough damage to notice or need control. The following profiles, in alphabetical order, feature the more common insects that create problems in Midwest lawns.

Ants

Formica and related species

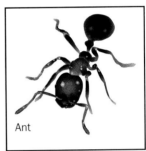

Ant

Favored Hosts: Unhealthy or stressed lawns.

Feeding Time: Throughout the summer, more troublesome in hot dry weather.

Overwinter As: All stages.

Harmful Stage: Nymphs (juveniles) and adults.

Life Cycle: The ant colony includes a queen, worker ants, eggs, legless larvae, and pupae. The worker ants forage for food and care for the queen. Some species of ants feed on seeds, insects, and other materials.

Insect Description: Ants measure from $1/32$ to more than $1/2$ inch and may be red, yellow, brown, or black. They have a narrow (constricted) waistline, may be winged or wingless, and have elbowed antennae. Ants live in colonies or nests usually located in the soil alongside a foundation or in the yard.

Damage Symptoms: Usually not harmful to the lawn. Ant hills can expose grass roots, resulting in desiccation and death of individual plants. Hills can cause uneven areas in the lawn, making mowing difficult or smothering surrounding grass. The ants are more of a nuisance to people and pets.

Scout and Count: Ants are more a nuisance than a turf health issue. Treat when the number or location of the mounds exceeds your tolerance level.

Management: Ants do not invade healthy lawns. Improve the health and quality of your lawn to rid your lawn of this nuisance. Treat ant hills and surrounding areas with an insecticide labeled for this use. Do not disturb the nest before treatment. Granules are most effective.

Armyworm

Pseudaletia unipuncta and related species

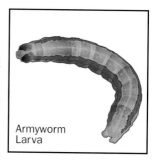

Armyworm Larva

Favored Hosts: Kentucky bluegrass, tall fescue. All lawn grasses can be at risk during severe outbreaks.
Feeding Time: Spring (April-June) and fall (August-October) and typically during the day.
Overwinter As: Usually larvae, though some species overwinter in the south, and the adult moths fly as far north as Canada to lay their eggs.
Harmful Stage: Larvae in soil, thatch, and debris.
Life Cycle: Dormant larvae resume feeding in the spring. They eventually return to the soil to pupate, change to adult moths that lay eggs, and start the cycle all over again. There can be several generations per season depending on the location and climate.

Armyworm Adult

Insect Description: Large pale green caterpillars with distinct yellow or brownish-green stripes. They are about 1$^1/_2$ inches long when fully grown. The larvae curl into a "C" when disturbed. The adult moths are dull pale brown to gray with a white spot in the center of each forewing. The eggs are greenish white, spherical, and laid in masses. The pupae are initially reddish brown, but turn almost black before they change into adults. Color varies among species.
Damage Symptoms: Individual leaf blades, as well as the root crowns, are chewed and eaten. With severe infestations, the lawn can develop circular bare spots.
Scout and Count: Rarely a problem, though severe damage can occur if there is an average of more than one per square yard. Use the irritation test in several locations to locate the pest and evaluate the severity of the infestation.
Management: The presence of the adult moth does not mean there will be a severe outbreak of the larvae. Diseases and predators of the larvae can keep their populations in check. Evaluate and adjust watering practices. Armyworms are more of a problem in well-watered lawns. If damage is severe or populations are high, use an insecticide labeled for controlling armyworms in the lawn. Mow, rake, and water before treating with sprays or granules. Do not water for at least three days after spray application.

Billbug

Sphenophorus species

Billbug Larva

Favored Hosts: Kentucky bluegrass, perennial rye-grass, and fescues mixed with bluegrass.

Feeding Time: Spring through fall.

Overwinter As: Adults hibernating in grass.

Harmful Stage: Adults and larvae.

Life Cycle: Adults emerge in spring, feeding on leaves and burrowing into the stems where they lay eggs. Larvae hatch and feed on grass stems and roots during the growing season before they change into adults in the fall.

Insect Description: About ³/₈-inch long, adults are black or brown beetles with a snout typical of a weevil. The larvae are also about ³/₈-inch long and resemble white grubs. Not as big as other grubs,

Billbug Adult

the billbug larvae are legless and white with yellowish or brownish heads. The pupae are pale yellow, almost white, and similar in shape to the adult.

Damage Symptoms: Most symptoms appear in summer when the grass is suffering from heat and drought stress. Small areas turn yellow, then brown, and the grass can eventually die. In these areas, the grass can be pulled out by hand and easily lifted from the soil where the chewing has occurred. A sawdust-like material called frass is usually present on the stem where chewing has occurred.

Scout and Count: Cut and lift sod in the area bordering the damage. Check the top few inches of soil for larvae. Treatment is needed if three to five grubs or ten adults are found per square foot.

Management: Treat only if damage is evident, the insect has been identified, and high infestation levels are reached. Treat adults in May. Mow and remove clippings before applying insecticide. Apply in early morning or late afternoon, and do not water or mow for three to four days after applying sprays. Treat larvae in July or August if they are found. Mow and remove clippings before applying insecticide. Water thoroughly immediately after treatment and before spray dries. Both sprays and granules are effective.

Chinch Bug

Blissus leucopterus hirtus montandon

Favored Hosts: Kentucky bluegrass, fine fescues, perennial ryegrass.

Feeding Time: Late June through August and into September.

Overwinter As: Adults in the thatch and bases of grass stems in the turf.

Harmful Stage: Nymphs (juvenile stage) and adults.

Life Cycle: Overwinter as adults. Female lays eggs in early spring. First generation matures in midsummer and lays eggs. Both adults and juveniles can be found feeding in mid- to late summer when the weather is hot and dry.

Insect Description: The eggs are bean-shaped, rounded on one end and blunt on the other and less than $1/32$-inch long. The immature chinch bug goes through five stages of growth and development called "instars." Major color changes occur in each stage with the head staying brown and abdomen changing from an orange to purple-gray to black. The adults are approximately $3/8$-inch long and gray-black. The wings are white with a black spot in the middle of the front wing.

Damage Symptoms: Chinch bugs feed at the base of tender leaves. The damage is usually first noticed when irregular patches of turf begin to turn yellow or straw color or die. Damaged areas continue to enlarge.

Scout and Count: Use the flotation test to find and identify chinch bugs. Damage will occur, and pest management is recommended when you find three to five bugs per test area.

Management: Well-watered turf and predominantly bluegrass lawns tend to resist chinch bug attacks. Seed or overseed with perennial ryegrasses, fine fescues, and tall fescues containing endophytes, which are highly resistant to this pest. Look for big-eyed bugs, a natural predator of the chinch bug, when doing the flotation test. They look similar to chinch bugs (except wider head with bulging eyes). These insects appear after the chinch bug populations have started to climb and damage is evident. So do not spray if these predators are present.

You may choose to use a chemical if your lawn has yearly problems with chinch bugs. A single application in May can provide season-long control. Otherwise, treat as needed with sprays or granules. Water thoroughly before treating with a spray formulation or lightly after applying granules.

Cutworm

Several species

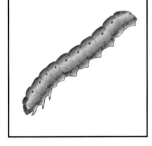

Favored Hosts: Kentucky bluegrass, fescue.

Feeding Time: Throughout the growing season; generally feeds at night or on cloudy days.

Overwinter As: Eggs; pupae; or mature, inactive larvae. Some species overwinter in the south and migrate north in the spring.

Harmful Stage: Larvae sever plant stems and roots.

Life Cycle: In spring, the overwintering forms turn into adults. Some moths migrate north from their wintering homes in the southern part of the country. The adult moths mate, and the females lay numerous eggs in clusters. The eggs hatch, and the worm-like larvae feed and grow. Several generations can occur in one season.

Insect Description: Adult moths are the "miller moths" you may remember from childhood. These brown moths are inactive during the day but are often attracted to lights at night. The juvenile stage, called a larva or caterpillar, reaches 2 to 3 inches. Some species are dull gray or white, and others may have stripes and distinctive coloring. They curl into a "C" when disturbed. The pupae are brown.

Damage Symptoms: Stems are chewed near the soil surface. The area wilts and turns brown and spotty.

Scout and Count: Use the irritation test to find and identify cutworms. Treatment may be needed when populations exceed one per square yard.

Management: Control is seldom needed unless symptoms are present and larvae numbers are high. Evaluate and adjust watering practices. Cutworms are more likely to be found in well-watered lawns. Mow, rake, and water before treating with sprays or granules. Do not water for at least three days after a spray application.

Greenbug

Schizaphis graminum

Favored Hosts: Bluegrass and fine fescue lawns in the southern parts of the Midwest.

Feeding Time: Summer.

Overwinter As: Eggs, though most overwinter in the south; once hatched, the juveniles blow north on the wind.

Harmful Stage: Nymphs (juveniles) and adults.

Life Cycle: Eggs hatch in spring. Most of these are females, which are able to give birth to live aphids (mostly female) without mating. There can be several generations each year.

Insect Description: Typical aphid, small, $1/16$ inch, pale green or yellow tear-drop shape with dark eyes and antennae

Damage Symptoms: Areas of discolored turf ranging from pale green to burnt orange and usually found under shade trees

Scout and Count: Examine leaf blades. Treatment may be needed when 30 greenbugs per blade are found.

Management: Natural predators such as ladybugs, rove beetles, and spiders usually keep these insects under control. Check for predators before treating. Spot-treat areas with high populations and no predators. Treat an extra 6 feet of healthy turf around the damaged area.

Leafhopper

Several species

Favored Hosts: Kentucky bluegrass, fine fescues, and perennial ryegrass lawns.

Feeding Time: Throughout the growing season.

Overwinter As: Eggs or adults in plant debris.

Harmful Stage: Nymphs (juveniles) and adults.

Life Cycle: Adults begin to feed and mate in the spring, laying eggs in the leaf blades of the grass. Two weeks later, the eggs hatch into nymphs that mature and grow into adults and repeat the cycle. There can be several generations a season.

Insect Description: Yellow, white, or green wedge-shaped insect $1/8$ to $1/4$ inch in size. The nymphs and adults jump when disturbed.

Damage Symptoms: Leafhoppers have needle-like mouthparts that pierce the leaf surface. The insects suck plant juices, causing the grass to wilt, yellow, and eventually appear bleached. Damage occurs in scattered areas or throughout the lawn.

Scout and Count: Trying to catch a leafhopper is like trying to catch a grasshopper. No treatment levels have been established. Treat when leafhoppers and damage are evident.

Management: Usually not harmful on established lawns and well-managed lawns. Improve the health of your lawn to control the problem. If damage is severe or a new lawn is attacked, use a pesticide labeled for controlling leafhoppers on the lawn.

Sod Webworm

*Pediasia trisecta (*syn. *Crambus trisecta)*

Favored Hosts: All lawn grasses.

Feeding Time: Spring through fall.

Overwinter As: All the sod webworm larvae spend the winter as a partially grown larva several inches below the soil surface.

Harmful Stage: Larvae.

Life Cycle: Varies depending on the species. All overwinter as larvae. There are one or two generations per season depending on the species. Larvae are present throughout the season. The sod webworm caterpillars live in tunnels constructed in the thatch layer or just below the soil surface. Adults appear in midsummer.

Insect Description: The moths vary depending on the species. In general, they are a dull, gray-brown with streaks at the base of the front wings. They fold their wings like a tent when resting, are weak flyers, and fly mostly at dusk near the soil surface. Eggs are tiny, oblong, and white to pale yellow. The larvae reach up to 1½ inches. They vary among species but are typically pinkish white to yellowish brown with coarse hairs and spots on each segment. Pupae are reddish-brown.

Damage Symptoms: The larvae usually feed at night, cutting the grass blades off just below the soil or thatch line and pulling them into their feeding tunnels at the soil surface. This causes the lawn to thin in these areas. Severe infestations result in irregular patches of brown grass. The symptoms are more obvious in hot dry weather.

Scout and Count: Peak activity is usually in late spring and late summer. Adult moths can be seen throughout most of the summer. Their presence doesn't mean the larvae are or will cause turf damage. Look at the soil surface for silk-lined tunnels that are a webby mix of soil and grass blades. Do the irritation test if you suspect sod webworms. Treatment may be needed if you have more than one webworm per square yard of grass.

Management: If damage is severe and high numbers are present, you may decide to treat. Use an insecticide labeled for controlling sod webworms in the lawn. Mow and rake before treating. Do not water for at least three days after a spray application.

White Grubs

Japanese beetle larva *(Popillia japonica)*
May or June beetle or bug *(Phyllophaga* spp.*)*

White Grub

Favored Hosts: All lawn grasses.
Feeding Time: Anytime during the growing season though damage is most evident during hot dry weather.
Overwinter As: Larvae (grubs) in the soil.
Harmful Stage: Larvae.
Life Cycle: Life cycle varies with the species and may be completed in one to three years. Most overwinter as larvae deep in the soil. The larvae move closer to the soil surface where they feed on the grass roots. The larvae pupate into adult beetles that feed above ground on other plants. The beetles mate and lay their eggs in the soil. Those larvae hatch, move deeper into the soil, and start feeding on the grass roots.
Insect Description: Japanese beetles are oval, about $7/16$- to $1/2$-inch long, with a metallic greenish-brown body. White hairs appear on the abdomen behind the wings. Patches of white are also located on each side of the body. May or June beetles have a slightly bigger, up to $3/4$-inch, oblong body. They are shiny, reddish-brown to

Japanese Beetle

May Beetle

almost black. The eggs are pearly white and oblong. Both larvae have brown heads and lighter colored bodies. The Japanese beetle larvae are whiter than those of the June beetle. Both can grow to 1 inch long; both typically rest in the "C" position.
Damage Symptoms: Grass roots are severed and eaten. Large areas of yellowing grass begin to brown and die. The grass can be easily lifted since the roots have been destroyed. Digging and damage by skunks, raccoons, and moles searching for a dinner of grubs are often the first signs of problems.
Scout and Count: Lift or remove sections of grass, roots and all, in the damaged areas. Treatment may be necessary if grub populations reach three to four per square foot of grass.

Management: Minimize the stress on your turf to help it withstand the damage better. Well-watered turf masks the symptoms but provides better conditions for the Japanese beetle grubs. The milky spore fungus is effective only on the larvae of Japanese beetles. Insecticides labeled for grub control on lawns will treat the larvae of both beetles. Incorporate insecticides into the soil of grub-infested lawns before seeding and sodding. Treat established lawns in late May or August through early September when the grubs are feeding near the soil surface.

Turfgrass Diseases

It starts as a small patch of brown grass that seems to expand and quickly take over your yard. If you are lucky, this hasn't happened to your lawn. If it has, you and your lawn were victims of circumstance. You just happened to be growing the right kind of grass (susceptible plant) when the environmental conditions were favorable for the disease, which just happened to be present in your lawn. All three factors must exist for the disease to harm your grass.

We can't change the weather, but we can select the most disease-resistant grasses and manage the lawn properly so when a disease-causing organism (pathogen) moves in, it has minimal impact on the lawn.

Just as you stay alert to insects and weeds, you must scout the lawn often for signs of disease. Catching a disease early may mean the difference between adjusting watering practices and replacing the entire lawn. Many diseases can be prevented or suppressed through management practices. Fertilizing in fall instead of early spring, watering in the morning instead of the evening, or mowing at the proper height can help alleviate some disease problems.

Cultural instead of chemical solutions are often the best cure for an outbreak of disease. Overseeding lawns with disease-resistant grass cultivars can give you long-term relief from such disease problems as melting out. Thinning the tree canopy or replacing grass with shade-tolerant ground covers eliminates powdery mildew on grass growing in the shade. Check your lawn often, and monitor changes in grass health, growing conditions, and your care. Early detection allows you to make quick and minor adjustments that will have a big impact on your lawn.

Proper Identification

I saved the diseases for last—they are the most difficult to identify. They "all look alike," with yellow or brown leaves in circular or irregular patches. Worse yet, they look like other problems, such as dog urine, salt damage, and wet soils. So where do you start? Use the questions in the Pest Problem Questionnaire and Troubleshooting Symptoms chart at the beginning of this chapter. The questions will help you evaluate the growing conditions and health of your lawn while the symptom chart will help you sort out the possible causes for the problem in your lawn.

Seek professional help if you can't identify the problem or want to confirm your diagnosis. Many University Extension offices provide this service free or for a minimal fee. Or visit your local garden center or landscape professional for assistance. Take any information you have gathered, along with a sample of the problem, to help them give you the best possible diagnosis. Dig a piece of grass, roots and all, from the edge of the diseased area. Make sure the sample includes both discolored and green turf. Symptoms are often easiest to spot on the grass blades growing next to the infested area. Send or deliver the sample to the experts as soon as possible. Package and transport the sample so the roots and tops stay moist without rotting. Avoid leaving the sample in a plastic bag in a hot car. It will be a smelly mess of dead grass that can't be identified. Consult your Extension Office for more details on collecting and mailing lawn samples.

Fungicides

Once you have exhausted cultural controls, you may decide to use a chemical to control the problem. Several fungicides are on the market and labeled for use on home lawns. Most of them are preventatives and won't cure what is already affected. These chemicals prevent the healthy grass from becoming infected. This protects the grass as it re-enters the damaged area. Several applications may be needed. Check the label for information on how and when to apply these products. Follow all the directions so you get the best possible results with the least risk to you, your lawn, and the environment.

Alternative Disease-Control Products

As more and more chemical fungicides are being pulled off the shelves, more environmentally friendly materials are being evaluated and introduced. Some of the vegetable oils, copper (a long-time favorite), and

Neem are a few products being used for disease control. Check the label before buying and using these products to be sure they will control your lawn's problem. Keep in mind that even when a label says "safe," the product may still harm your plants, you, or the environment if it is misused. Avoid home concoctions that are not research based. These "under-the-sink" remedies can burn and even kill your lawn. They are also very expensive if you start adding up the cost to treat the whole lawn. Contact a professional before reaching for the disinfectant, beer, or floor cleaner.

Common Lawn Diseases

Brown Patch
Rhizoctonia solani

Grasses at Risk: Kentucky bluegrass and fescue.

Season of Occurrence: Summer.

Environmental Conditions Needed: Extended periods of hot humid days and nights; most prevalent on improperly watered and over-fertilized lawns.

Spread By: Moisture and wind.

Symptoms: Small, 4-inch diameter, brown circular areas appear suddenly in the lawn and increase in size with hot humid weather. The outer edge of damage is a darker gray, giving it a "smoke ring" look. Foliage turns water-soaked, then gray, and finally brown. Small tan lesions may occur at the soil line. Grass looks wilted and can easily be pulled from the base of the plant.

Can Resemble: Dog damage and white grubs.

Management: Adjust fertilization program, avoiding excess nitrogen in spring and during the disease period. Water thoroughly, less frequently, and early in the day. Using a sharp blade, mow the lawn when it is dry. Control thatch. Badly infested lawns can be treated with a fungicide. Use one labeled for controlling brown patch on lawns. Treat affected and adjoining areas.

Dollar Spot

Formerly *Sclerotinia homeo-carpa,* now thought to be a combination of *Moellerodiscus* and *Lanzia* species

Grasses at Risk: Kentucky bluegrass.
Season of Occurrence: Spring through fall.
Environmental Conditions Needed: Stressed lawns from drought and improper fertilization are at greatest risk. Mild drought with heavy morning dews and warm (but not hot) weather are conducive to this disease.
Spread By: Foot traffic, mower tires, splashing water, or wind.
Symptoms: Lawns may appear drought-stressed with uneven growth. Small, 2-inch diameter, bleached circular areas appear throughout the lawn. The spotting gave it the name dollar spot. The spots may coalesce to form larger patches several feet across. Individual leaf blades have spots with distinct tan margins.
Can Resemble: Dull mower blade, drought, dog damage, and pythium.
Management: Water early in the morning, deeply and infrequently. Mow when the grass is completely dry. Adopt a fertilization program using the right type and amount of fertilizer. Control thatch. If necessary, use a fungicide labeled for controlling dollar spot on home lawns.

Fairy Ring

Several fungi

Grasses at Risk: All lawn grasses.
Season of Occurrence: Spring through fall.
Environmental Conditions Needed: No significant weather pattern but affected turf may die during dry periods.
Spread By: Mycelium (part of the fungus) growth in the soil and spores spread by water and wind.

Symptoms: Rings of dark green, sometimes yellow or brown, grass appear in the lawns. They may disappear for part of the season but return later that season or next. The rings get slightly larger with each occurrence. Occasionally mushrooms will sprout along the edge of the ring. One or more rings can appear in the lawn. Fairy ring is an eyesore for some but not a threat to the health of your lawn.

Can Resemble: Fairly distinct.

Management: Core aerate to increase water and fertilizer penetration in affected areas. Add a commercial wetting agent or mild dishwashing detergent to help water and fertilizer penetrate the fungal mat. Proper watering and fertilization reduce the symptoms but do not eliminate the disease. Some gardeners have tried removing and replacing the soil. You must remove all the soil 12 inches below and several inches beyond the ring. If any contaminated soil touches the ground, you have re-infected the lawn. ProStar fungicide is registered for controlling this problem.

Fusarium Blight Syndrome or Necrotic Ring Spot

Leptosphaeria korrae

Grasses at Risk: Kentucky bluegrass and fine fescues. Recently sodded lawns, two to seven years old, appear more susceptible.

Season of Occurrence: Throughout the seasons.

Environmental Conditions Needed: Newly established lawns and those with a dense stand of grass or thatch problems are at risk. Symptoms are often more evident during dry periods preceded by wet weather.

Spread By: Splashing water, wind, and foot traffic.

Symptoms: Several patterns of damage may be seen. Affected lawns may have 6- to 15-inch circles of brown grass with a tuft of green grass in the middle. Or there may be large patches of brown grass with several tufts of green grass scattered throughout. The crowns, roots, and rhizomes may show distinct brown or red lesions.

Can Resemble: Summer patch, brown patch, and pythium.

Management: Control thatch, water properly, and avoid excess fertilization. Overseed the lawn with perennial ryegrass for visual relief. This disease seems eventually to run its course. I have seen treated and untreated lawns end up looking the same after several years. Patience and proper care is the best treatment.

Helminthosporium Leaf Spot

Formerly known as *Helminthosporium,* now thought to be *Bipolaris* and *Dreschslera* species

Grasses at Risk: Kentucky bluegrass, fine fescues, and ryegrass.

Season of Occurrence: All season, though most prevalent in spring and fall.

Environmental Conditions Needed: Most common in moist cloudy conditions.

Spread By: Wind, water, mower, and shoes.

Symptoms: Grass starts out looking thin and weak. Irregular areas turn brown, and the grass just seems to disintegrate or "melt out." A closer look will reveal brown or purple lesions with a distinct darker margin. The crowns and lower stems turn purple or brown. Finally, the roots rot, creating a shallow-rooted turf that eventually "melts away."

Can Resemble: Drought stress, though leaf spots and melting out symptoms are distinct.

Management: Proper maintenance provides the best control. Cut the grass high, water thoroughly but less frequently, avoid excess fertilizer in spring, and control thatch. Overseed with resistant bluegrass cultivars such as 'Adelphi', 'Baron', 'Eclipse', 'Majestic', 'Nugget', 'Parade', and 'Touchdown'. Lawns suffering severe and frequent outbreaks may be treated with a fungicide labeled for this disease. Read and follow all label directions.

Powdery Mildew

Erysiphe graminis

Grasses at Risk: All lawn grasses.

Season of Occurrence: Anytime but most common in spring and fall.

Environmental Conditions Needed: Shade, poor air circulation, fluctuating humidity, and mild temperatures.

Spread By: Moisture, wind, and foot traffic.

Symptoms: A white powdery substance covers the leaves. The lawn looks like someone sprinkled baby powder on it. Infected leaves can eventually turn yellow and brown from lack of sunlight.

Can Resemble: Slime mold and chemical residue, but symptoms are fairly distinct.

Management: Overseed with more shade-tolerant fine fescues. If the problem persists, you may have to replace the turf with a more shade-tolerant ground cover or increase the light by thinning out the trees. Contact a certified arborist who can do the job properly and safely. Treatment usually is not needed. Chemicals will provide immediate control, but if the cause (shade and poor air circulation) is not corrected, the disease will return.

Pythium Blight, Grease Spot, or Cottony Blight

Pythium aphanidermatum and related species

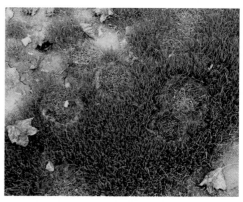

Grasses at Risk: All lawn grasses.

Season of Occurrence: Midsummer.

Environmental Conditions Needed: Warm temperatures over 85 degrees Fahrenheit; high humidity; and wet foliage from dew, rainfall, or irrigation. Over-fertilized and over-watered lawns growing in shady areas with poor air circulation are more susceptible.

Spread By: Movement of contaminated soil and water runoff.

Symptoms: The lawn may appear water-soaked. Then tan or brown spots or patches appear and quickly collapse. A cottony growth may be seen on the dew-covered grass in the morning. Leaf blades are water soaked, grayish-green, and shriveling; they eventually turn brown. The grass has a slimy look and feel.

Can Resemble: Dollar spot or dog damage.

Management: Improve drainage, increase air circulation, and water thoroughly but less frequently. Avoid excess fertilization, which encourages lush growth that is more susceptible to disease. Avoid mowing and walking on wet turf.

Rust

Puccinia species

Grasses at Risk: All lawn grasses; ryegrass most susceptible.

Season of Occurrence: Late summer through fall.

Environmental Conditions Needed: Newly seeded (with a high percentage of ryegrass) or poorly managed lawns are most susceptible. The disease is most common during cloudy weather, moderate drought, and mild temperatures.

Spread By: Wind and splashing water.

Symptoms: Orange shoes when you walk across the lawn. A closer look reveals yellow flecks on the grass leaves that become orange and fuzzy. The whole lawn may have a yellow or reddish cast.

Can Resemble: Nutrient and moisture problems.

Management: Not a serious disease, rust will diminish on new lawns as the bluegrass and fescue become established and outnumber the more rust-prone ryegrass. Evaluate and correct fertilization and watering practices. Healthy turf with moderate, not excessive, growth is less likely to be infected. Chemical control is seldom needed. Apply only registered fungicides to lawns with a history of rust where cultural controls have not been effective.

Slime Mold

Several fungi

Grasses at Risk: All lawn grasses.
Season of Occurrence: All seasons.
Environmental Conditions Needed: Prolonged rainy periods.
Spread By: Wind and splashing water.
Symptoms: Looks like someone splattered white paint on the lawn. The leaves initially are covered with white or creamy flecks that turn a distinctive purplish, ash-gray, looking almost sooty. Small or large areas may be affected. The disease does not harm the grass and usually disappears once drier weather returns. Any damage that occurs is from extended coverage for long periods. In these cases, the slime mold prevents the sunlight from reaching the grass, causing it to yellow.
Can Resemble: Powdery mildew.
Management: None is usually needed. The mold will disappear once drier weather returns. If the mold persists, wipe it off with a broom or cloth or wash it off with a strong blast of water.

Snowmold

Typhula species and
Microdochium nivalis

Grasses at Risk: Ryegrass most susceptible; bluegrass in extreme conditions.
Season of Occurrence: October through April.
Environmental Conditions Needed: Heavy snow falls or ice covering non-frozen turf over winter or late-winter snowstorms.
Spread By: Moisture.
Symptoms: Areas of matted grass appear as the snow line recedes. Matted grass is most common where snow was piled or lingered due to shade. The matted

grass may be covered with a cobweb-like growth. Affected areas may have a pinkish or gray cast.

Can Resemble: Winterkill.

Management: Lightly rake the grass as the snow recedes. This helps dry the surface and encourage new growth. In late fall, apply fertilizer to improve recovery of turf if damage occurs. Reseed damaged areas to speed recovery. Improve drainage if this is a regular occurrence. Chemical controls are usually not needed since the damage is done by the time you see the symptoms.

Environmental Problems

Chlorosis

Grasses at Risk: All lawn grasses.

Season of Occurrence: Throughout the growing season.

Environmental Conditions Needed: Poor fertility or extremely high pH. Iron and manganese are bound to high pH soils and unavailable to plants. Extremely high pH soils may cause grass to yellow and lose vigor due to a lack of these nutrients. Insufficient nitrogen can also cause yellowing.

Symptoms: Grass blades tend to turn a light green to yellow green, especially on new growth. Older leaf blades may be yellow with dark green veins. Vigor is poor, and there is no sign of disease or insects.

Can Resemble: Some diseases, improper watering, nematodes.

Management: Have your soil tested to determine nutrient levels and pH. Adjust your fertilization program and soil pH as recommended. Topdressing with organic matter and leaving clippings on the lawn help moderate soil pH. Use acidifying fertilizers such as ammonium sulfate or add elemental sulfur to lower pH. Always follow soil test recommendations. Improper use of these products can damage the lawn.

Dog Damage

Grasses at Risk: All lawn grasses.

Season of Occurrence: All year, whenever the dog is present.

Environmental Conditions Needed: A lawn and a dog, especially female.

Spread By: The dog.

Symptoms: Dark green and brown spots scattered throughout the lawn. The urine has high nitrogen content and acts like a fertilizer. Too much in one spot burns the lawn.

Can Resemble: Brown spot and dollar spot.

Management: Train the dog to use one section of the lawn where damage is not a concern or create a mulched area where the urine will not cause damage. (This may not be practical if your dogs obey you as well as my cats listen to me.) Water the area right after the dog urinates. This dilutes the urine and minimizes or eliminates damage. I have had mixed reports on the urine-neutralizing products. You may be just as successful with water. Or contact your veterinarian. There are some pills you can give your dog that makes the urine less harmful to the lawn, but there are mixed reports on effectiveness.

Lumpy Lawns

Grasses at Risk: All lawns.

Season of Occurrence: All seasons.

Environmental Conditions Needed: Lumpy lawns can be a result of poor grading and soil management when seeding and sodding lawns. Anthills and earthworm activity can also cause lumps and bumps in the grass.

Symptoms: Lawn looks fine but ground is uneven and feels lumpy under your feet. In extreme cases, scalping of the lawn due to uneven soil surface occurs.

Can Resemble: Distinct in appearance.

Management: Topdress the lawn, filling in low spots. The existing turf will grow through the thin layer of topsoil. Overseed thin areas at the same time. See the ant profile for tips on managing these pests. Do **not** kill earthworms. They are nature's aerators and help improve the soil, drainage, and health of your lawn. Lots of earthworm activity means your lawn is healthy. Just consider the lumps a bit of an inconvenience for all the benefits they provide. If I haven't convinced you of their value, I do have a suggestion for co-existence. Use an empty roller on the lawn when the soil is moist (not wet). This helps flatten out the lumps without killing the worms. Repeat as needed.

Salt Damage

Grasses at Risk: All lawn grasses.

Season of Occurrence: Damage occurs over winter, symptoms appear in spring.

Environmental Conditions Needed: De-icing salts applied to streets, walks, and drives that end up in the grass.

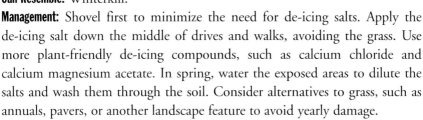

Spread By: People.

Symptoms: Brown areas of grass along walks, drives, and roadways.

Can Resemble: Winterkill.

Management: Shovel first to minimize the need for de-icing salts. Apply the de-icing salt down the middle of drives and walks, avoiding the grass. Use more plant-friendly de-icing compounds, such as calcium chloride and calcium magnesium acetate. In spring, water the exposed areas to dilute the salts and wash them through the soil. Consider alternatives to grass, such as annuals, pavers, or another landscape feature to avoid yearly damage.

Shade

Grasses at Risk: Kentucky bluegrass, all grasses in dense shade.

Season of Occurrence: During the growing season.

Environmental Conditions Needed: Trees and buildings.

Symptoms: Grass begins to thin and may disappear. Shade-tolerant weeds or moss moves in to the bare areas. Competition for water and nutrients from the shade-producing trees may add to the turf decline.

Can Resemble: Nematodes and most pest problems.

Management: Use a more shade-tolerant grass. Fine fescues will tolerate dry shade while supina and rough bluegrass will tolerate moist shade. See Chapter Six for more information on these grasses. Raise the mowing height and adjust fertilization for shady conditions. If this doesn't work, consider replacing the grass with shade-tolerant ground cover or mulch. As a last resort, hire a certified arborist to thin out the dense canopies of the shade-producing trees.

Other Problems

Moles

Grasses at Risk: All lawns can be damaged by tunneling.

Season of Occurrence: Summer, moles hibernate for winter.

Environmental Conditions Needed: Well-drained or sandy soils, high populations of grubs (moles' favorite food), insects, and soil that is easy to dig.

Symptoms: Ridges in the lawn and a pile of soil at the tunnel exit, creating a heart-shaped molehill. Moles do not feed on the grass. They eat the insects that live in the soil. Their tunneling can result in an uneven surface and disturb the grass roots. Moles are dark brown, furry, and about 3 inches long.

Can Resemble: Moles are often blamed for vole damage.

Management: Look at moles as a natural grub and insect control. They do you a favor by eating these troublesome pests. If you can't tolerate their damage, you can try to eliminate the food source. But you'll have to wait for the insects to die—and you may kill a lot of beneficial insects in the process. Gas cartridges are available from garden centers. Read and follow all directions, and do not use them under or next to buildings. MoleMed has been shown to be effective in Michigan. Choker and harpoon traps can be used to trap and kill these animals. These traps look as gruesome as they sound.

Nematodes
Several species

Grasses at Risk: All lawn grasses, though rarely a problem in Midwest lawns.

Season of Occurrence: Summer.

Environmental Conditions Needed: Stressed grass, warm weather, and drought.

Spread By: Can move short distances in soil and water but are usually moved in on shovels, equipment, and feet.

Symptoms: Small sections or the whole lawn may appear stunted and pale. The lawn's overall growth and vigor are affected by the root feeding. Damaged roots are not able to withstand drought, cold, or heat stress. The nematodes overwinter in the egg stage. In spring, as the soil warms to 50 degrees Fahrenheit, the eggs hatch into adults. The adults are microscopic but feed aggressively on the grass roots, reducing their depth and density. There will also be an absence of normal healthy white feeder roots. The symptoms appear in summer when the grass is heat and drought stressed. Weeds, especially the nematode-resistant sedges and spurges, start to move into the thinned turf. If you can see the "worm" feeding on your grass roots, it isn't a nematode. You need special equipment and training to diagnose this problem. Have your soil checked for nematodes before treating your lawn. Contact your local Extension Service for guidelines on collecting and submitting a sample.

Can Resemble: Drought, nutrient deficiency, and decline caused by some diseases.

Management: Add organic matter to improve the water-holding capacity of sandy soils and drainage in heavy clay soils. Incorporate these materials whenever starting or renovating a lawn. Proper mowing, fertilization, and watering can make lawns more resilient if attacked by these and other pests. Spreading colloidal phosphate ground into sand or ground crab shells, sold as chitin, has helped reduce nematode populations. Soil sterilants and nematicides are available but can be applied only by licensed professionals. Or try replacing your lawn with a cover crop or other nematode-resistant plant. This could be a short-term solution until the nematodes die (from lack of food), or it could be a long-term alternative to the traditional lawn. Who knows, you may start a new trend in the neighborhood.

Voles or Meadow Mice

Grasses at Risk: All lawn grasses.

Season of Occurrence: Voles feed on seeds and plants year round. Lawn damage is most evident in spring as the snow recedes.

Environmental Conditions Needed: Long grass and high vole populations (three hundred to one thousand per acre).

Symptoms: Trails of worn and disturbed grass. Voles are similar to, but smaller than, field mice. They scurry under the snow in search of seeds, roots, and tree bark to eat. Trails are worn into the grass by voles' high numbers and constant travel.

Can Resemble: Moles are often blamed for their damage.

Management: Repair lawn damage in spring. Gently tamp disturbed grass back in place. The surrounding grass will fill in small damaged areas of turf. Overseed larger areas to speed recovery. Hawks, skunks, owls, foxes, and weasels are vole predators and can help keep their populations under control. Or use snap traps baited with oats and peanut butter. Tuck these in areas safe from kids, pets, and other wildlife.

Table 3.1

Common Organic Lawn Fertilizers and Analyses

Material*	% Nitrogen (NO$_3$ or NH$_4$)	%Phosphorus (P$_2$O$_5$)	%Potassium (K$_2$O)	Availability
Basic Slag[1]	-	8-11	-	slow-medium
Blood Meal	15.0	1.3	0.7	slow
Bone Meal	4.0	21.0	0.02	slow
Compost (unfortified)[2]	2.5	0.08	1.5	slow
Cottonseed Meal	7.0	1.3	1.2	slow
Dried Blood	12-15	3.0	-	medium-fast
Fish Emulsion	5.0	-	-	medium-fast
Fish Meal	8.0	7.0	-	slow
Greensand[3]	-	1.5	5.0	slow
Guano (bat manure)	12.0	-	-	medium
Hoof Meal/Horn Dust	12.5	1.8	-	slow
Kelp (seaweed)	1.7	0.8	5.0	slow
Leaves (pulverized)	0.9	0.2	0.3	slow
Manure (cattle)	2.0	1.0	2.0	medium
Manure (horse)	0.4	0.2	0.3	medium
Manure (poultry)	3-5	2-3	1-2	medium
Manure (sheep)	0.6	0.3	0.2	medium
Milorganite[4]	6.0	2.0	0.0	medium
Mushroom Compost	1.8	0.6	2.2	slow
Peat/Muck	2.0	0.5	0.8	slow
Soybean Meal	6.7	1.6	2.3	slow-medium
Wood Ashes[5]	-	1-2	3-8	fast

*Nutrient levels can vary widely depending on source and manufacturer

[1] Mineral by-product of the steel industry

[2] Unfortified means no synthetic or additional fertilizer was added during the composting process

[3] Mined under-sea deposits with many trace minerals

[4] Processed biomass microorganisms from sludge

[5] Very fine alkaline material; avoid using on alkaline and clay soils

Some organic sources attract wildlife that can dig in and damage your lawn.

Table 3.2

Recommended Fertilizer Amounts

Do math functions make your head spin? Here is a bit of a cheat sheet to help
you calculate your fertilizer needs.

Fertilizer Analysis	Fertilizer Ratio N-P-K	Amount of fertilizer needed per 1000 square feet to apply:	
		½ lb actual Nitrogen	1 lb actual Nitrogen
45-0-0	1-0-0	1.1	2.2
33-0-0	1-0-0	1.5	3.0
27-7-7	3-1-1	1.9	3.7
24-8-16	1-1-2	2.1	4.2
21-0-0	1-0-0	2.4	4.8
20-20-20	1-1-1	2.5	5.0
19-19-19	1-1-1	2.6	5.2
18-6-12	3-1-2	2.8	5.6
16-8-8	2-1-1	3.1	6.2
15-15-15	1-1-1	3.3	6.7
12-12-12	1-1-1	4.2	8.3
10-10-10	1-1-1	5.0	10.0
6-12-12	1-2-2	8.3	16.6
6-2-0	3-1-0	8.3	16.6
5-10-5	1-2-1	10.0	20.0

This is not a complete list. Select the fertilizer with the ratio (N-P-K) that best fits your soil test recommendation. Or use the following calculation:

100 divided by %N in fertilizer times the actual nitrogen needed per 1000 square feet = amount of fertilizer needed per 1000 square feet

For example, if you use urea with an analysis of 45-0-0 and soil test recommends 1 pound of actual N per 1000 square feet, you would need:

$$\frac{100}{45} \times 1 = 2.2 \text{ pounds of fertilizer per 1000 square feet}$$

Table 5.1
Ground Cover Suggestions

Tired of a garden full of green? Select ground covers that add seasonal interest to the landscape. Use ground covers with variegated foliage to brighten shady locations, while flowering types can be used to add color throughout the season. Add some that have colorful leaves in the fall, or evergreen foliage and attractive seedheads for winter.

Ajuga:	Select one of the bronze or variegated cultivars for added color. Flowers in spring are typically blue, but some cultivars are white or pink.
Creeping Phlox:	Covered with white, rose, or purple flowers in spring. The evergreen foliage provides year-round cover.
Deadnettle:	Green leaves with various amounts of silvery white variegation. Mauve or white flowers in late spring to early summer stand above the foliage.
Hosta:	Many cultivars of various sizes with green, chartreuse, or blue-green foliage are available. Some have white, cream, or yellow variegation. White and purple flowers in summer or fall are considered an added benefit by gardeners. Some have fragrant flowers.
Moneywort:	Bright yellow flowers cover the green leaves in summer. Use the less assertive, yellow-leaved variety for a colorful change.
Orange Stonecrop:	Covered with yellow-orange flowers in summer; the foliage turns yellowish orange in fall.
Pachysandra:	White flowers in April with glossy green evergreen foliage.
Variegated Yellow Archangel:	Variegated green and silver foliage with yellow flowers in late spring to early summer. An aggressive plant that tolerates dry shade.
Wintercreeper:	Low-growing evergreen ground cover; the foliage turns purple in winter.

Table 5.2
Calculating Plant Quantities

Determine planting bed area: (width x length = square feet)

Recommended Spacing (inches, from center to center)	Number of Plants (per square foot)
6	4.00
8	2.25
10	1.44
12	1.00
18	0.44
24	0.25

Table 5.3
Perennial Ground Covers for Shade

Common Name	Other Name	Botanical Name	Cold Hardiness Zones	Comments
Ajuga	Bugleweed	*Ajuga reptans*	3-9	creeps into lawn
Archangel		*Lamium galeobdolan*	4-8	less invasive cvs.
Barren Strawberry		*Waldsteinia ternata*	3-8	can be aggressive
Barrenwort		*Epimedium*	3-9	moist, organic soils
Bearberry		*Arctostaphylos uva-ursi*	2-6	moist, acid soils
Bishop's Weed		*Aegopodium podagraria*	3-9	can be invasive
Bunchberry		*Cornus canadensis*	2-7	acid, cool temps.
Coral Bells		*Heuchera* spp.	4-8	attractive foliage and flowers
Daylily		*Hemerocallis*	3-10	repeat bloomer, dry
Dead Nettle		*Lamium maculatum*	4-8	tolerates dry shade
English Ivy		*Hedera helix*	4-8	can be invasive
Euonymus	Wintercreeper	*Euonymus fortunei*	4-9	can be invasive
Ferns		(Assorted species)	2-10	moist, organic soils
Foam Flower		*Tiarella cordifolia*	3-7	moist, slightly acid
Ginger, Canadian		*Asarum canadense*	2-8	tolerates dense shade
Ginger, European		*A. europaeum*	4-8	winter burn in north
Hosta		*Hosta*	3-8	easy, wide variety
Houttuynia		*Houttuynia cordata* 'Chameleon'	5-11	aggressive, moisture tolerant
Japanese Spurge	Pachysandra	*Pachysandra terminalis*	4-8	yellows in excess winter sun
Leadwort	Plumbago	*Ceratostigma plumbaginoides*	6-9	borderline hardy in Zone 5
Lilyturf		*Liriope muscari*	5-10	borderline Zone 5
Mazus		*Mazus reptans*	5-9	flowers late spring
Mondo Grass		*Ophiopogon japonicus*	6-10	protection in Zone 5
Partridge Berry		*Mitchella repens*	4-9	acidic soil
St. John's Wort		*Hypericum calycinum*	5-9	2 ft. tall
Sweet Woodruff		*Galium odoratum*	4-8	fragrant flowers
Vinca	Periwinkle	*Vinca minor/major*	4-9	can be invasive

Sample Grass Seed Label

Premium Shade Grass Mix

Percent	Ingredient		
	Fine Fescues	Germination	Origin
23.00	Jamestown chewings	87%	Washington
20.50	Dawson creeping red	85%	Washington
10.00	Nordic hard fescue	90%	Washington
	Kentucky Bluegrass		
15.00	Adelphi	85%	Oregon
15.00	Eclipse	85%	Oregon
	Perennial Ryegrass		
7.50	Citation III	90%	Washington
7.50	Pennfine	90%	Washington
Other Ingredients:			
1.30	Inert Material		
0.10	other crop seed		
0.05	weed seed		
0.00	noxious weed seed		

Tested: month, year

Net Weight: X pounds

Green Grass Seed Company

Midwest, USA

Lot Number: #####

Kentucky Bluegrass Cultivars

Able — NR

Adelphi — NR, HLS

Admiral — NR

Allure

Alpine

America — LM, NR

Aspen

Banff

Barblue — LM

Barmax

Baron — HLS

Barzan — NR

Blacksburg — HLS

Bluechip — LM

Bristol

Caliber — LM

Challenger — NR

Cheri

Chicago — LM

Classic — NR

Columbia

Coventry

Cynthia

Eagleton

Eclipse — NR, HLS

Freedom — NR

Glade — NR

Haga — NR

Julia — LM

Kelly — NR

Liberator — LM, HLS

Limosine — HLS

Livingston — LM

Majestic — NR, HLS

Midnight — NR, HLS

Monopoly — LM, NR

Nasau — LM, NR

NuBlue — LM

Nugget — HLS

Parade — LM, HLS

Plush — LM

Ram I — LM

Rambo — LM

Rugby — NR

Rugby II — LM, HLS

Shamrock

SR 2000 — NR

SR 2100

Sydsport

Trenton — NR

Unique — LM

Vantage — NR

Victa — LM

Wabash — LM, NR

Washington

LM — good for low maintenance lawns
NR — resistant to Necrotic Ring Spot
HLS — resistant to or tolerant of Helminthosporium Leaf Spot

Chewings Fescue Cultivars

Ambassador — LM

Banner III — LM, HLS

Bridgeport

Intrigue — LM

Jamestown

Jamestown II

Sandpiper — LM

Shadow II — LM, HLS

Shadow E — Endo

SR5100

Tiffany — LM

Treazure — LM, HLS

Victory

LM — good for low maintenance lawns

HLS — resistant to or tolerant of Helminthosporium Leaf Spot

Endo — seed contains endophytic fungus that increases the plant's vigor as well as drought and stress tolerance

Creeping Red Fescue Cultivars

Aruba

Dawson — LM

Jasper II — LM, Endo

Seabreeze — LM, HLS

LM — good for low maintenance lawns

HLS — resistant to or tolerant of Helminthosporium Leaf Spot

Endo — seed contains endophytic fungus that increases the plant's vigor as well as drought and stress tolerance.

Hard Fescue Cultivars

4001 — LM, DS

Atilla — LM, DS

Aurora — Endo

Bighorn — LM

Defiant — LM

Discovery — LM, DS, HLS

Heron — LM, DS

Minotaur — LM

Nordic — LM, DS

Osprey — LM, DS, HLS

Reliant II — LM, DS, HLS

Rescue 911 — LM, DS

Scaldis — LM

SR3100 — HLS

LM — good for low maintenance lawns

HLS — resistant to or tolerant of Helminthosporium Leaf Spot

DS — Dollar Spot resistant or tolerant

Endo — seed contains endophytic fungus that increases the plant's vigor as well as drought and stress tolerance

Sheep Fescue Cultivars

Azay — LM

Quatro — LM, DS

LM — good for low maintenance lawns

DS — Dollar Spot resistant or tolerant

Tall Fescue Cultivars

Amigo	Maverick II
Apache	Monarch
Avanti	Olympic II
Aztec	Phoenix
Bonanza	Rebel II
Chieftain	Shenandoah
Crossfire	Thoroughbred
Eldorado	Tribute
Guardian	Wrangler
Hubbard 87	

Turf-Type Perennial Ryegrass Cultivars

Advent	Gettysburg
Allaire	Manhattan II
APM	Manhattan II — Endo
Barage	Omega II
Barry	Ovation
Blazer II	Pinnacle
Brenda	Repell II
Caliente	Saturn
Dandy	Seville
Diplomat	SR4200
Elka	Tara
Express	Target
Gator	Yorktown III

Endo — seed contains endophytic fungus that increases the plant's vigor as well as drought and stress tolerance

Weights, Measures, and Calculations for Lawn Care

Linear Measure:

12 inches = 1 foot

3 feet = 1 yard

5,280 feet = 1,760 yards or 1 mile

Area Measure:

144 square inches = 1 square foot

9 square feet = 1 square yard or 1,296 square inches

1 acre = 43,560 square feet or 4,840 square yards

640 acres = 1 square mile

Cubic Measure:

Square feet times inches deep divided by 324 = cubic yards

1,728 cubic inches = 1 cubic foot

27 cubic feet = 1 cubic yard

1 bushel = 1.25 cubic feet

1 cubic foot = 0.8 bushel

7.48 gallons = cubic foot

2,150.42 cubic inches = 1 standard bushel

231 cubic inches = 1 standard gallon (liquid)

1 cubic foot = 7.48 gallons

Spreading bulk material like mulch or soil:

	3 Cubic Foot Bag	2 Cubic Foot Bag	1 Cubic Foot Bag
1/2 inch deep	covers 72 square feet	covers 48 square feet	covers 24 square feet
1 inch deep	covers 36 square feet	covers 24 square feet	covers 12 square feet
2 inches deep	covers 18 square feet	covers 12 square feet	covers 6 square feet
3 inches deep	covers 12 square feet	covers 8 square feet	covers 3 square feet

3 Cubic Foot Bag

Depth of Product	100 Square Feet	1,000 Square Feet
2 inches	6 bags	60 bags
3 inches	9 bags	90 bags
4 inches	11 bags	110 bags

2 Cubic Foot Bag

Depth of Product	100 Square Feet	1,000 Square Feet
2 inches	8 bags	80 bags
3 inches	12 bags	120 bags
4 inches	15 bags	150 bags

Weights, Measures, and Calculations
for Lawn Care

Coverage in Square Feet	Square Feet	Inches Deep
1 cubic yard	1,944	1/8 inch
1 cubic yard	1,296	1/4 inch
1 cubic yard	648	1/2 inch
1 cubic yard	324	1 inch
1 cubic yard	162	2 inches
1 cubic yard	108	3 inches
1 cubic yard	81	4 inches
1 cubic yard	54	6 inches
1 cubic yard	40	8 inches
1 cubic yard	27	12 inches

Dry Measure:

2 pints = 1 quart (qt.)

(= 67.2006 cubic inches)

8 quarts = 1 peck (pk.)

(= 637.605 cubic inches or 16 pints)

4 pecks = 1 bushel (bu.)

(= 2550.4 cubic inches or 32 quarts)

1 (short) ton = 2,000 pounds (lbs.)

1 (long) ton = 2,240 pounds (lbs.)

Liquid Measure:

Teaspoons (tsp.)

3 tsp. = 1 Tbs.

Tablespoons (Tbs.)

2 Tbs. = 1/8 cup or 1 fluid ounces (fl. oz.)

4 Tbs. = 1/4 cup or 1 fl. oz.

8 Tbs. = 1/2 cup or 1/4 pint

16 Tbs. = 1 cup or 1/2 pint

Cups, pints, quarts

2 cups = 1 pint or 16 fl. oz.

2 pints = 1 quart

4 quarts = 1 gallon

Watering Your Lawn:

To cover 1,000 square feet with an inch of water takes 625 gallons

One gallon per minute (gpm) = 1,440 gallons per day

10.4 gallons per minute applies one inch of water over 1,000 square feet every hour

Gallons/minutes × 8.03 = cubic feet per hour

One gallon of water weighs 8.34 pounds

Weights, Measures, and Calculations for Lawn Care

More Conversions:

Multiply	To Obtain
bushels by 0.8	cubic feet
bushels by 0.04545	cubic yards
cubic feet by 1.2	bushels
cubic feet by 0.03704	cubic yards
cubic feet by 1728	cubic inches
cubic inches by 0.00002143	cubic yards
cubic inches by 0.0005787	cubic feet
cubic yards by 22	bushels
cubic yards by 27	cubic feet
cubic yards by 46.656	cubic inches
feet by 12	inches
feet by $1/3$	yards
pounds by 16	ounces

Metric Conversions:

Area

1 square foot = 0.093 square meters

1 square yard = 0.836 square meters

1 acre = 4.047 square meters

1 square mile=2.590 square kilometers

Weight

1 pound = 0.454 kilograms

1 ton (short) = 0.907 metric tons

1 ton (long) = 1.016 metric tons

Volume

1 cubic foot = 0.028 cubic meters

1 cubic yard = 0.765 cubic meters

Capacity

1 quart (liquid) = 0.946 liters

1 quart (dry) = 1.101 liters

1 gallon (liquid) = 3.785 liters

1 bushel = 35.239 liters

Length

1 inch = 2.54 centimeters

1 foot = 0.305 meters

1 yard = 0.924 meters

1 mile = 1.609 kilometers

Glossary for Lawn Care

Acid soil: soil with a pH less than 7.0. The lower the pH the more acidic or "sour" the soil. Soils are acid when concentrations of bases like calcium and magnesium are low in relation to hydrogen and aluminum. This can occur naturally in forested areas or as a result of leached soils or growing crops. Sulfur is typically added to the soil to make it more acidic.

Aeration: the process of punching holes in the soil to increase the amount of oxygen available to plant roots and correct compaction problems.

Alkaline soil: soil with a pH greater than 7.0. The higher the pH the more alkaline or "sweet" the soil. Sometimes referred to as "basic" soil because it has high concentrations of bases as opposed to acids. Lime is typically added to the soil to make it more alkaline.

All-purpose fertilizer: powdered, liquid, or granular fertilizer with a balanced proportion of the three key nutrients—nitrogen (N), phosphorus (P), and potassium (K). Often used for maintenance nutrition for most plants.

Amendments: components added to soil to improve fertility or texture.

Annual: a plant that lives its entire life in one season. It is genetically predetermined to germinate, grow, flower, set seed, and die the same year. Some plants that are perennial in their native habitats, but not hardy in another region, such as tropical plants, can also be used as annuals.

Beneficial insects: insects or their larvae that prey on pest organisms and their eggs, or benefit the garden in another way. They may be flying insects, such as ladybugs, parasitic wasps, praying mantids, and soldier bugs, or soil dwellers such as predatory nematodes and ants. Spiders and earthworms are considered beneficial also although they are not technically insects.

Berm: soil raised above ground level to create height in the landscape or provide better drainage for a particular planting.

Broadleaved: plants having leaves of wider breadth in relation to length and thickness, in contrast to grassy plants. Broadleaved, or broadleaf, weeds are typically dicots, whereas grasses are monocots. Dicots and monocots respond differently to chemical controls.

Bt: abbreviation of *Bacillus thuringiensis*, an organism that attacks a certain stage in the life cycle of some pests. Forms of Bt can be created to target a particular species. Used as a natural pest control.

Canopy: the overhead branching area of a tree, usually referring to its extent including foliage.

Chlorotic: yellowing of leaves either from pest or nutrient problems.

Clumping: a contained growth habit versus a spreading growth habit.

Cold hardiness: the ability of a plant to survive the winter cold in a particular area.

Compaction: when soil particles are packed so tightly together that air and water cannot easily penetrate.

Complete fertilizer: containing all three major components of fertilizers—nitrogen (N), phosphorus (P), and potassium (K), although not necessarily in equal proportions. An incomplete fertilizer does not contain all three elements.

Compost: organic matter that has undergone progressive decomposition by microbial and macrobial activity until it is reduced to a spongy, fluffy texture. Added to soil of any type, it improves the soil's ability to hold air and water and to drain well.

Cool-season grass: turfgrasses that prefer and thrive in cooler northern conditions. They can remain green during milder winters.

Coring: the act of mechanically removing small plugs of soil from the ground, allowing for better penetration of oxygen and water to alleviate soil compaction, and also providing lodging places for new grass seed. Can be used as part of maintenance program or done in preparation for renewing an established lawn or installing a new one. Also called core aeration.

Crown: the base of a plant at, or just beneath, the surface of the soil where the roots meet the stems.

Cultivar: a CULTIvated VARiety. It is a naturally occurring form of a plant that has been identified as special or superior and is purposely selected to carry on this trait.

Deciduous plants: trees and shrubs that lose their leaves in the fall.

Desiccation: drying out of foliage tissues, usually due to drought or wind.

Dethatching: the process of raking or removing the mat of partially decomposed remnants of grass parts lodged at the soil surface, beneath the living grass layer. Can be done manually or mechanically; vertical mowing (or verti-cutting) is one method.

Dicot: shortening of the word "dicotyledon." Plant with two cotyledons or seed leaves emerging from its seed, such as a bean or an acorn. Also includes such weeds as dandelion, violet, and clover.

Division: the practice of splitting apart plants to create several smaller-rooted segments. The practice is useful for controlling the plant's size and for acquiring more plants.

Dormancy: or dormant period. Time during which no growth occurs because of unfavorable environmental conditions. For some plants it is in winter, and for others summer. Many plants require this time as a resting period.

Drought tolerant: plants able to tolerate dry soil for varying periods of time. However, plants must first be well established before they are drought tolerant.

Established: the point at which a newly planted tree, shrub, flower, or grass begins to produce new growth, either foliage or stems. This is an indication that the roots have recovered from transplant shock and have begun to grow and spread.

Evergreen: plants that do not lose all of their foliage annually with the onset of winter. They do, however, shed older leaves at certain times of the year while retaining younger leaves, depending on the species.

Foliar: of or about foliage, usually referring to the practice of spraying foliage, as in fertilizing or treating with pesticide. Leaf tissues absorb liquid directly for fast results.

Fungicide: a pesticide designed to destroy or prevent fungus.

Genus: a distinct botanical group within a family, typically containing several species. Plural form is "genera," referring to more than one genus.

Germinate: to sprout. Germination is a fertile seed's first stage of development.

Grading: changing the slope of the land, usually to make it more level or a more gradual incline.

Hardscape: the permanent, structural, non-plant part of a landscape, such as walls, sheds, pools, patios, arbors, and walkways.

Heat tolerance: the ability of a plant to withstand the summer heat in a particular area.

Herbaceous: plants having fleshy or soft stems, with very little woody tissue, as opposed to woody plants. Herbaceous and woody plant stems differ structurally, in that herbaceous plants undergo little or no secondary growth, while woody plants do.

Herbicide: plant-killing material designed to kill or prevent unwanted plants (weeds).

Humus: partially decomposed organic matter.

Hybrid: a plant that is the result of intentional or natural cross-pollination between two or more plants of the same species, genus, or family.

Insecticide: a pesticide for killing insects or preventing their damage.

Integrated Pest Management: a combination of pest management techniques used to reduce the need for pesticides. Also referred to by the acronym IPM.

Invasive: when a plant has such a vigorous growth habit that it crowds out more desirable plants.

Irrigation: manmade systems of pipes, sprinkler heads, and timers installed to provide supplementary water to landscaping.

Leaching: the removal of nutrients from the soil by excessive amounts of water.

Life cycle: stages in the life of an organism. With insects it is important to know the cycles of both beneficial and harmful ones, since different stages vary in their locations, vulnerabilities, and eating habits.

Micronutrients: elements needed in small quantities for plant growth. Sometimes a soil will be deficient in one or more of them and require a particular fertilizer formulation.

Monocot: shortening of the word "monocotyledon." Plant with one cotyledon or seed leaf emerging from its seed, such as with corn or grass.

Mowing strip: a type of barrier placed between the lawn and landscaped areas that accommodates lawnmower tires, making it easier to mow the lawn edge neatly, and preventing ruts or compaction to the edges of the beds.

Mulch: a layer of material over bare soil to protect it from erosion and compaction, and for moisture retention, temperature control, weed prevention, and aesthetics.

Mulching mower: mower that chops grass blades into small pieces.

Node: structure on a stem from which roots, leaves, and other branches arise.

Non-selective: herbicides that have the potential to kill or control any plant to which they are applied.

Nutrients: elements available through soil, air, and water, which the plant utilizes for growth and reproduction.

Organic material, organic matter: any material or debris that is derived from living things. It is carbon-based material capable of undergoing decomposition and decay.

Overseeding: spreading new grass seed on an established lawn to thicken the grass coverage or introduce another type of grass to extend the season of green.

Partial shade: situation with filtered or dappled sunlight, or half a day of shade.

Pathogen: the causal organism of a plant disease such as fungus, bacteria, or virus.

Peat moss: organic matter from peat sedges (United States) or sphagnum mosses (Canada), often used to improve soil texture. The acidity of sphagnum peat moss makes it ideal for boosting or maintaining soil acidity while also improving its drainage.

Perennial: a plant that lives over two or more seasons. Many die back with frost, but its roots survive the winter and generate new shoots in the spring.

pH: a measurement of the relative acidity (low pH) or alkalinity (high pH) of soil or water based on a scale of 1 to 14, 7 being neutral. Individual plants require soil to be within a certain range so that nutrients needed can dissolve in moisture and be available to them.

Plug: piece of sod used in establishing a new lawn. Plugs can also be grown or purchased in small cells or pots within a flat, sometimes referred to as trays.

Pollen: the yellow, powdery grains in a flower. A plant's male sex cells, they are transferred to the female plant parts by means of wind, insects, or animal pollinators to fertilize them and create seeds.

Pre-emergent: an herbicide applied to the soil surface to prevent weed seed from germinating.

Post-emergent: an herbicide applied to already germinated and actively growing weeds to kill or control them.

Reel mower: a type of mower generally thought of as old fashioned, but with updated versions achieving renewed popularity. Blades are arranged horizontally in a cylinder, or reel, that spins, cutting the grass blades against a metal plate.

Renovation: renewing an established lawn, partially or completely.

Rhizome: a swollen energy-storing stem structure, that lies horizontally in the soil, with roots emerging from its lower surface and growth shoots from a growing point at or near its tip, as in bluegrass and quack grass.

Rotary mower: a mower with its blades arranged in a pinwheel under the body of the mower, which cuts by the high speed of the spinning blades.

Runner: horizontal stem that grows along the soil surface and forms plantlets at each node. An example is the strawberry.

Runoff: when water moves across the landscape without being absorbed, because the slope is steep, the volume of water is greater than the absorption capacity of the soil, the soil is compacted, or the surface is of an impenetrable material. Runoff from areas that have had chemicals applied can cause problems in the areas ultimately receiving the water.

Selection: a variation within a species that occurs naturally due to the presence of a multitude of genetic possibilities. Over several generations plants with the desired characteristic are isolated and propagated. This process has been particularly important in agriculture.

Selective: pesticide that targets a particular type of weed or pest.

Self-seeding: the tendency of some plants to sow their seeds freely around the yard. Can create many seedlings the following season that may or may not be welcome.

Semi-evergreen: tending to be evergreen in a mild climate but deciduous in a rigorous one.

Shade tolerant: a plant's ability to maintain health and continue growth in a shaded location.

Slow-acting fertilizer: fertilizer that is insoluble in water, designated as slow release or controlled release, and releases its nutrients gradually as a function of soil temperature, moisture, and related microbial activity. Typically granular, it may be organic or synthetic.

Sod: commercially grown turfgrass sections cut from a field in rectangular panels or rolls, used to establish new lawns. The standard size is $1^1/2$ ft. × 6 ft. (9 sq. ft.).

Soil conditioner: chemical or organic material which aggregates soil particles for improved structure.

Species: a group of fundamentally identical plants within a genus. Synonymous with the more botanically accurate designation "specific epithet."

Sterile: producing no viable seeds or spores, and in lawn grasses no flowers, which is an advantage since the flowers are typically taller than the leaf blades and are not attractive. The disadvantage is that such grasses cannot be bought as seed, only as sod, sprigs, or plugs.

Stolon: horizontal stem that grows along the soil surface. It can form plantlets at the tips of the stems. An example is the blackberry.

Synthetic: products made to imitate a natural material, as in synthetic fertilizer or pesticide.

Tamp: pressing down on newly installed sod so that the roots have good soil contact. This can also be achieved by "rolling" by which a heavy cylindrical drum is rolled over the sod.

Thatch: layer of undecayed grass found between the soil surface and the living grass blades.

Threshold: the level at which a pest becomes harmful to its target host plant. Lower levels of the pest might not warrant treatment.

Topdressing: the act of applying granular products such as fertilizer, lime, compost, topsoil, etc. over the top of lawn grass.

Topsoil: the fertile layer of soil where plant roots grow. Sometimes the naturally occurring topsoil is inadequate for certain plants, or has been removed during construction, in which case it might be necessary to purchase topsoil from a local supplier.

Translocation: movement of water, minerals, food, or chemicals within the plant.

Transpiration: water loss by evaporation from external leaf surfaces.

Transplanting: moving plants from one planting location to another.

Turf: grass used to make a lawn.

Turfscaping: wise use of turf in the overall landscape.

Variety: a group of plants within a species which have stable characteristics separating them from the typical form. Frequently used synonymously with cultivar and selection, even though there are differences in the definitions of the three terms.

Vegetative: non-sexual production of plant material typically achieved by divisions or cuttings and not as a result of flowering, pollination, and seed formation.

Vertical mowing: the mechanical act of cutting into a lawn vertically with sharp blades or tines to lift dead vegetation such as thatch. Also called verti-cutting.

Viability: refers to seed that is healthy and able to germinate.

Warm-season grass: turfgrasses that thrive and perform in warm southern conditions. They can go dormant during the coldest parts of the winter, then resume growth in the spring.

Water-logged: soil that holds too much water for most plants to thrive, associated with poor aeration, inadequate drainage, or soil compaction.

Weed: a plant growing where it is not wanted.

Weed-and-feed: a product that combines fertilizer and pre- or post-emergent weed killer.

White grubs: fat, off-white, wormlike larvae of beetles. They reside in the soil and many types feed on plant (especially grass) roots until later in the season when they emerge as beetles.

Bibliography

Dobbs, Steve. *The Perfect Oklahoma Lawn.* Nashville, TN: Cool Springs Press, a Division of Thomas Nelson, Inc., 2002.

Fizzell, James. *Month-by-Month Gardening in Indiana.* Franklin, TN: Cool Springs Press, 1999.

Fizzell, James. *Month-by-Month Gardening in Illinois.* Franklin, TN: Cool Springs Press, 1999.

Fizzell, James.*Month-by-Month Gardening in Michigan.* Franklin, TN: Cool Springs Press, 1999.

Iowa State University Extension publications, on-line at http://www.extension.iastate.edu/pubs/

Michigan State University Extension publications, on-line at www.msue.msu.edu

Myers, Melinda. *Month-by-Month Gardening in Minnesota.* Franklin, TN: Cool Springs Press, 2001.

Myers, Melinda. *Month-by-Month Gardening in Wisconsin.* Franklin, TN: Cool Springs Press, 2001.

Purdue University Extension Service publications, on-line at http://www.agcom.purdue.edu/AgCom/Pubs/menu.htm

Stier, John. *Lawn Maintenance and Establishment.* Madison, WI: University of Wisconsin Extension, Cooperative Extension Service, 2001.

Stier, John. *Lawn Maintenance and Problems.* Madison, WI: University of Wisconsin Extension, Cooperative Extension Service, 2001.

Ohio State University Extension publications, on-line at http://ohioline.osu.edu/

University of Illinois Extension publications, on-line at http://www.urbanext.uiuc.edu/

University of Minnesota Extension publications, on-line at www.extension.umn.edu

University of Wisconsin Extension publications, on-line at www.uwex.edu/ces/wihort/

University of Missouri Outreach and Education publications, on-line at http://muextension.missouri.edu/xplor/agguides/hort/

Index

Meet the Author

Melinda Myers, best known for her gardener-friendly and practical approach to gardening, has over twenty years of horticultural experience in both hands-on and instructional settings. She has a Masters Degree in Horticulture and is a Horticultural Instructor at Milwaukee Area Technical College, where she teaches students preparing to work in the field of landscape horticulture. Outside the classroom, Myers shares her expertise through a variety of media. She hosts "Great Lakes Gardener" seen on PBS stations throughout the Midwest. She has hosted the "Plant Doctor Radio Show" on WTMJ since 1987. Past shows include "Wisconsin Lawn and Garden," a weekly show on PBS, "Yardworks," a nationally syndicated yard care and garden show, and a variety of other cable gardening programs.

Myers is also an accomplished garden writer. She has been contributing editor and columnist for *Birds & Blooms Magazine,* a publication with two million subscribers throughout the United States and Canada, since 1996 and written a bi-monthly column, "Gardeners' Questions," for the *Milwaukee Journal* since 1986. Myers has written several books, including *The Garden Book for Wisconsin, My Wisconsin Garden: A Gardener's Journal, Month by Month Gardening in Wisconsin, Minnesota Horticultural Society's Minnesota Gardener's Guide,* and *Month-by-Month Gardening in Minnesota.*

Her thirteen years experience at the University of Wisconsin Extension Service allowed her to work with backyard, community, and master gardeners throughout Wisconsin. As Milwaukee's Assistant City Forester, Myers helped manage the street trees, boulevards, and green spaces for the city. She has worked with the Young Adult Conservation Corps supervising crews that maintained University of Wisconsin urban test gardens, repaired hiking trails, and other conservation work. A horticultural consultant to numerous community and beautification groups, Melinda began the Master Garden Program in Milwaukee County.

For her work and media presence Myers has received recognition and numerous awards including the 1998 Garden Communicator's Award from the American Nursery and Landscape Association and the 1998 Quill and Trowel award from the Garden Writers Association of America.

Lawn Notes

Lawn Notes